Earth Tones

Praying the Psalms with All Creation

Pamela Smith

EarthTones

*Praying the Psalms
with All Creation*

TWENTY-THIRD PUBLICATIONS

185 WILLOW STREET • PO BOX 180 • MYSTIC, CT 06355
TEL: 1-800-321-0411 • FAX: 1-800-572-0788
E-MAIL: ttpubs@aol.com • www.twentythirdpublications.com

Dedicated to

the Mergels,
Gina Moskal,
the Religious Sisters of Mercy of Pittsburgh,
and the staff of the Mercy Center at Madison

The Scripture passages contained herein are from the *New Revised Standard Version of the Bible*, copyright © 1989, by the Division of Christian Education of the National Council of Churches in the U.S.A. All rights reserved.

Twenty–Third Publications
A Division of Bayard
185 Willow Street
P.O. Box 180
Mystic, CT 06355
(860) 536-2611 or (800) 321-0411
www.twentythirdpublications.com
ISBN:1-58595-320-2

Library of Congress Catalog Card Number: 2003113501
Printed in the U.S.A.

Contents

Introduction

The late Dom Helder Camara, in reflections published after his retirement from office as archbishop of Recife, Brazil, wrote: "The psalms teach us to lend our voice to all creatures: to the mountains and the waters; to the trees and the birds; to the light that comes from above and to the earth that provides for us; to the creatures of the sea, from the tiniest fish to the whale" (*Sister Earth*, 29).

From its beginnings, the tradition of the *habiru*—the Semitic wanderers who, from desert and rocky gardens, from the Jordan River and the Sea of Reeds, from mountain smoke and burning bush, wrought a people, a land, a destiny, and a conviction that God is one—has been an earthy tradition and an earthy religion. The religion of the people who became Israel insisted that God must be met in the here and the now, that love must be celebrated in the present moment rather than hoped for in a misty hereafter, that children must be treasured and taught, and that gleanings and grapes must be left for the dispossessed.

When this people envisioned and erected its "Dwelling Place," its tabernacle, its meeting tent for the worship of God, it loaded it—almost to giddy excess—with the sensory, the sensual, the signs and symbols and things themselves that studded a resplendent world. The ephod and the breastplate alone summoned "gold, silver, and bronze; blue, purple, and crimson yarns, and fine linen; goat's hair, tanned rams' skins, and fine leather; acacia wood, oil for the light, spices for the anointing oil and for fragrant incense, and onyx stones and gems to set..." (Ex 35:5–9).

The lampstand that stood before the ark of the covenant bore images of almond blossoms (Ex 37:17–22). The robe of the ephod was ringed with figures of bells and pomegranates (Ex 39:24–26). An array of precious stones bedecked the breastplate, and fine incense swirled its scents around the tabernacle. The tabernacle itself was surrounded by cloud and fire (Ex 40:38).

For the people Israel, the holiest of places must also be a revelry of things of Earth. It was a reminder that their great God "I Am" was giver of all creation and that true worship must be thanks, praise, and a return of gift. A dynamic of beauty received, beauty embraced, and beauty released was at the heart of Israel's adoration.

When this people collected its book of songs and prayers, its poems and processionals, its only book addressed entirely to God, the book could be nothing, then, but honest, energetic, and natural. The psalms of David, of Korah, of the Asaphites, the hymns of leaders and singers, of footbeat and glissaded strings: these prayer poems express longing, fear, love, triumph, need, hope, vengeance, pain, glory, gore, abandonment, and gratitude. The psalms sigh and sing with a human voice—human in the full stretch of wonder and emotion—and so too, since the human is, par excellence, earthling, with an earthen voice. There is no psalm that can be sung by a disembodied spirit, no psalm that can spring from some vague existential ether. No, the psalmist stands in grit and wades in water, lifts eyes and outstretched arms to night's stars, kneels grieving over blood and death, reclines eating, lies listening to the breathing of a lover, settles against the trunk of a tree lulled by the chitterings of night creatures and watching the sparks in the sky. Whether in wild outcry or in gentle thanks, the psalmist presents the human heart to God—*cor ad cor loquitur*—in company with "everything that breathes" (Ps 150:6).

The Psalms for Us

It doesn't require a clairvoyant to observe that all of us—modern, post-modern, whatever we fancy ourselves—are ever threatened by our drastic dissociation from the rhythms of seasons, the timings of sunrise and sunset, the phases of the moon, the bursts of mating among wildlife, the germinations and quiescence of vegetation. We can traverse the stores and business offices of downtown Minneapolis in mid-January via skywalks. We can conjure up all manner of fruits and vegetables from our grocery lanes all year round. We can work 24 hours a day under full light and in the botanical gardens—real, plastic, or silk—that many of our restaurants and workplaces have become. We have lit our cities, our highways, our airports so well that we have to set out for some wooded north country if we wish to see the comet of the century or merely catch a glimpse of Orion.

Disconnected from nature itself, we have also created a secular consumer culture that has whacked away at our sense of the sacred and left us bereft of the touch of God. So we weave loon cries and wolf howls eerily into our New Age music in the hope that it will slow us and wake some primeval memory. We collect crystals and sometimes gaze into them, waiting expectantly for some momentous truth. We drum and jet ski, agonizing for life pulse or a splash of water.

And some of us go back to old things, the trusty canoe or the log house or the old growth forest or the simple psalm, and find them new. These old things bear within them something of the pristine and indeed something of the godly.

As Helder Camara has suggested, the psalms give voice not only to the human longing for God and the good life but also to the godliness inherent in the rich nonhuman creation that surrounds us. In an age which must become what Thomas Berry calls "ecozoic," the psalms speak the truth about us and our world. They lay bare our human violence and incompleteness and aspiration and need. They remind us that the human is a creature among creatures—sometimes ornery, sometimes articulate, sometimes in harmony, sometimes all askew, but always kin to hyssop and dogs and stars and stones amid which we sing.

A Personal Note

Throughout the 1990s, I gave over considerable time and energy to the study of environmental issues. My doctoral dissertation, *Aquinas and Today's Environmental Ethics* (Duquesne, 1995), considered the theology of creation and the theory of the cardinal virtues in Thomas to see how these might provide a foundation for, and dialogue partner to, contemporary environmental ethical thought. A subsequent book, *What Are They Saying About Environmental Ethics?* (Paulist, 1997), and several convention presentations since (for the College Theology Society and the Society of Christian Ethics) have come from my forays into recent discussion of the "intrinsic value" and "moral considerability" of nonhuman creatures, the demands upon human virtue, and the religious response to questions of creation and ecojustice. Early in 1998 I became a member of the Board of Directors of the East Michigan Environmental Action Council, an organization which awakened me to the complex interaction of social-political structures and the ecosystems of the Great (and many smaller) Lakes.

Meanwhile, I have observed a certain hypocrisy in myself—one which besets not a few environmental thinkers. I continue to consume more than the bare minimal amounts of fuel, meat, fabric, paper, and plastic. I continue to pray at times as if there were no beings other than the divine and the human. And I continue to wish the institutions in which I live and work were more ecocentric, more Earth reverent, more abstemious, and more attuned to the trees that crash down and the grassy fields that get overlaid with asphalt to keep our church offices, our academic centers, our health care facilities, and our motherhouses in business. I think about all this as I continue guzzling coffee, often having forgotten to bring my own mug.

In Michigan, however, I found that I could at least continue something that began in my childhood, during summers at the Jersey shore: taking long pauses to watch water and attend to the cry of birds, to listen to the crunch of snow and catch the sound of a cricket or nutcracking squirrel as I stroll along a bank or beach. I have climbed down paths to waterfalls, paused for a long time at the edges of great lakes like Huron and Superior, and paddled in a small one called Minnewanna. Now that I am back in Pennsylvania, nestled in the hills and mountains that line the Susquehanna, I continue to watch in prayer for the occasions when the world-with-us, that whirl of land and sea, flying and swimming creatures, flowers and wind, calls me to attention and proclaims God-with-us.

The late Notre Dame theologian Catherine Mowry LaCugna, in her great work on the Trinity, spoke of "God for us." As I invite others to mosey through the psalms with me and to attend to what and who among creatures share our company, I hope that we can notice together that the "us" whom God is revealed to be "for" includes not only the multiracial, multiethnic, multi-religious world of women and men who have spanned the ages but also the world of Lebanon cedars and Palestinian goats, the world of desiccated streams and thunderous whirlwinds.

If we are people of prayer, we ought eventually to become better at living. I hope that the psalm-stimulated reflections which I share here help all of us to live more fully, more attentively, more reverently, and more inclusively as we honor being at large.

1.

Water Sources

Happy are those...[whose] delight is in the law of the Lord, and on his law they meditate day and night. They are like trees planted by streams of water, which yield their fruit in its season, and their leaves do not wither. **Ps 1:1–3**

Weeping willows so need water, they say, that they will wrap their roots around underground water pipes and drive through them to satiate their thirst. They flourish when they spring, thick and tall, on the banks of farm ponds and lush creeks, and their long, leaning, earth-lapping leaves bounce and green where there is water, water.

There is so much water that we need. We need the real water of placenta and our own buoyant bodies merely to exist on the planet. We need the waters of rivers and streams, pools and fountains and faucets in order to endure. And we need the symbolic waters of caring voices, loving touch, clear guidance, good teaching to immerse us in healthfulness and wisdom. We need, in other words, the rich resources of nature, nurture, and supernature if we are to yield fruit and not wither. By adulthood perhaps we begin to know that God can fall upon us, literally or figuratively, in drizzle or cloudburst. But forever after, and day by day, we learn and relearn our need to look under the squish of moss and morning dew for the deep-well places that refresh us, the mountain springs, the subterranean streams. Just to live, we will need to drink from these.

Where, then, do we find our water sources? Our spirit selves have the lesson, of course, of the Samaritan woman who met Jesus at Jacob's well (Jn 4): God is living water and lasting refreshment. But how do we drink of God in a way that is not purely ethereal, abstract, disembodied, or even imaginary? In liturgy and in personal prayer, of course, and in the living word of Scripture. But we also imbibe the water that enables us to bear fruit and to remain unwithered in the sensible, tangible earthiness of our friends and the richness of nonhuman creation. The flow of the waters themselves, the waves of ocean, and the ripples of windswept pools and lakes, the running of creeks quench us and wash us with life. There is good reason why we sing "Wade in the Water" for baptism and "Water of Life" for asperges rites, for sprinkling. There is wisdom in our natural impulses to sit or stand on the shore and watch an ocean for a long time or to walk slowly along the banks of river, creek, or lake when we are distraught, dismayed, or off kilter. There is something healing about water, whether we wash, wade, or watch.

So too with the trees, whose xylem and phloem pump water to the tips of branches to make blossoms and fronds and leaves.

And we ourselves are largely water, as we laugh or think, as we weep or eat, as we clear our throats and raise our voices to the God who is both of and above the sky.

Great God of still pools and white water, every day drench me and quench me with life. Drench me with the desire to seek your law at work in streams and trees, and let me see. Quench me with your word written in everything that moves and breathes. And remind me of the daylong goods and the many life sources that wash all around and through me.

For Reflection

- Where have I found "living water" today, and what beauty have I paused to drink in lately?
- What natural waterways have been comfort and strength for me?

2.

All Good Gifts

You have put gladness in my heart more than when grain and wine abound. **Ps 4:7**

Whether it is a Thanksgiving dinner that draws eleven people for a reunion over white wine, dark meat, drumsticks and gravy, seasoned stuffing and whipped potatoes, stuffed celery, olives, and pickled watermelon rind, topped off with a dessert of pumpkin pie, or whether it is a lavishly celebrated eucharist with tasteful music, bright lights, colorful processions, and communion under both species, we all are somehow gladdened by the color and kin, the loveliness and the lingering, the festive finery and the fine food that are of the essence of our holidays and festal liturgies.

These fiestas of heart and hearth always have something to do with God. They are all in some sense holy days. What we may miss, even as we are immersed in them, is the way in which these feasts not only use but celebrate the gifts and the fruits of the Earth. The food and the flatware, the vessels and the vestments, the candles and the arrangements of flowers and nuts and gourds are not merely everyday and functional. They are to be savored and lingered over. The unhurried look and the unhurried taste are fitting and opportune. We enjoy and say some kind of grace.

As much as 3000 years ago a psalmist remarked on the many who pray for a glimpse of goodness and God-light (Ps 4:6). He then remarked on his own sense of well-being, safety, and gladness in the assurance of God's presence, even when "distress" or disaster threatened. He could think of grain and wine and peaceful sleep. When we pause, as we do on splendid occasions, we can somehow relish the fact that day after day we walk and speak and eat and sleep. We suddenly remember that we are surrounded by the beauties of our landscapes, shelters, other people, beverages, breakfast cereals, salads, soups, pasta, beans and rice, fish, fowl and fresh fruit. We have blankets and beds and lights for the night. Birds twitter, dogs bark, cats slink around our houses, squirrels scurry up and down our trees. All of these are gifts. But generally we have been preoccupied or vexed and have hardly noticed. We have chowed down our meals from brown bags and drive-thru restaurants and listened to radio tunes without knowing what we've heard. We may have muttered a word or two to God, but our attention has been on other matters.

Eventually, however, these celebrations do come around, and we slow our pace and lower our guard.

"Love calls us," says poet Richard Wilbur, "to the things of this world." When we take these festive pauses, we remember love. And thus we recall the blessedness of familiar things. The best idea, we may think, would be to freeze or still these moments on and on, into some everlastingness. But what might be more possible, and more realistic, would be for us to find the feast in each day, the hidden banquet moment, to note it with gratitude, and count it as blessing.

If we are wishing for graciousness, goodness, and God-light, the secret is in our daily seeing. It may be that the abundance and graciousness and rest we seek are in what we ordinarily look at, hear, smell, taste, touch—in the very air we breathe.

God of natural gifts and simple things, show me when my open hands and my eager pleas are already filled. Give me a spirit that celebrates every goodness, everything that gives life.

For Reflection

- The spirituality of Francis of Assisi is marked by the recognition of the Creator in the creature. How often do I have the Franciscan gift of joy in nature and "the things of this world"?
- The Christian and the Buddhist mystical traditions have at their heart an emphasis on being present to the present. When do I find myself particularly absent (absent-minded, out of touch, distracted, disconnected)? What helps me to focus, to be present and attentive?

3.

Sky Gazing

When I look at your heavens, the work of your fingers, the moon and the stars that you have established, what are human beings that you are mindful of them? **Ps 8:3–4**

Blaise Pascal spoke in his *Pensées* of the frightfulness of the silent, cosmic immensity. Astronauts have testified to their awestruck wonder at this "blue planet," this rare Earth of ours, as they have seen it amid great emptiness and great, orbiting otherness. It is hard to feel anything but infinitesimal—as if our love and hate, our sanctity and our crime must be utterly inconsequential—when a galactic perspective flashes upon us. And yet, it seems that we do matter, even by the mere fact that we are observing the cosmos. We clock sunrises and sunsets. We mark our own calendars, our tides, and sometimes our mental states by moon phase. We trace imaginary lines from star to star and name these constellations: twins and dippers, bears and ancient Greek gods. We choose a comet, a meteor shower, a morning or evening star and call it "ours." We design space probes and build observatories and telescopes to study and chart the expanses of our universe and to detect the earliest remnant particles of the Big Bang. And, ironically, in an age of science we continue to publish horoscopes. Somehow we seek to unlock the mysteries of our past, our present, and our future in the skies.

Thomas Berry, the priest and ecological advocate who calls himself a "geologian," has noted that we humans are the universe and its processes come to consciousness. We do not know what other intelligences, if any, might occupy the millions and billions of light-years' distant planets splashed in multiplicity and splendor through the thus-far silent space. We do know, however, that we have intelligence. Thus we can wonder about our origins, make moral evaluations and aesthetic appraisals of our present state, and invest ourselves in planning and hoping for a future. We can think of and name and dream of visiting the far, great lights that stud our sky. And we can conceive of a divine and timeless being beyond the breadth and depth of everything.

We are made of Earth and cosmic dust. We are quite dependent and very small. Our lives are virtual milliseconds when we measure our time over against the cosmic clock. Yet somehow we persist in the belief that we have been thought of by Someone. The lights above and beyond us at night suggest to us the existence of uncharted and unchartable great Being. And, so far as we know, we are the only ones who seem to be thinking of and speaking in our hearts to that One Who Is.

God of unimaginable vastness, give me, even while I stand overwhelmed with my smallness on a night shore, the gift of endless gratitude for the simple fact that I am. Light my way, night and day. And illumine me with reverence for the universe and with praise.

For Reflection

- When I recall that, from a scientific point of view, our universe is expanding, how often do I note that I am expanding with it?
- How long has it been since the night sky has evoked wonder and praise from me? When will I look and remark on it again?

4.

Dominion

You have put all things under their feet, all sheep and oxen, and also the beasts of the field, the birds of the air, and the fish of the sea, whatever passes along the paths of the seas. **Ps 8:6–8**

In 1967, a now famous essay by Lynn White, Jr., appeared in *Science* magazine. White looked at the mounting evidence of environmental destruction—the pollution, the toxicity, the erosion, the decline and fall of species—and accused the Judaeo-Christian tradition of being not only aider and abettor but also prime culprit in our planetary waste-making. The problem, White suggested, was this notion of "dominion," verbalized in Genesis and here in the psalms: the idea that humans were called to direct, use, and dominate the creature-world. What that "dominion" led to, White argued, was exploitation, devastation, and death. Rational creatures were given a religious excuse, it seems, for treating the rest of creation unreasonably.

White's accusation has to be taken seriously. We might want to object that irreligious materialism, industrialism, capitalism, technocracy, and consumerism bear much blame. Yet we have to admit that it has been altogether too easy to read the command to "fill the earth and subdue it," to "have dominion over the fish of the sea and over the birds of the air and over every living thing that moves upon the earth" (Gen 1:28) as a license to use and manipulate. The notion that God has "put all things under their feet" (Ps 8:6) suggests all too readily that all else must be subservient to humans, submissive even to their kicking and trampling.

But "dominion" can and should, it seems, mean something altogether different from abuse. The "dominion" of a landlord or a tenant farmer indicates a realm of cultivation, care, and flourishing. No one certainly would desire "dominion" over a wasteland. "Dominion" implies a certain authority, but authority for the more enlightened need not imply power over but instead power for. Roy May, writing from the perspective of Costa Rican experience, argues as much. "Dominion" can be exercised as *ecologia mayordomica*, a caretaker's ecology of power for. Whether we think of that power for as power on behalf of God or power on behalf of everything around, above, and underfoot, it seems that we somehow must remember that human power is exercised vis-à-vis a creation that has been deemed "good." Propagating and diversifying are celebrated in the biblical vision. It seems reasonable to regard human "dominion" as power on behalf of the Creator and of all creation together, ourselves included. Such power can be advocacy for abundance, richness, beauty, plenty—in skies, seas, and soil.

There is a way of regarding what is "underfoot" (as this psalm has it) with wisdom, forbearance, and reverence. We keep off grass and flowerbeds, and we avoid stepping on a dog's or a cat's tail. We mow around the baby rabbits' nest. We rock in our chairs cautiously if a baby is crawling nearby on the carpet. We sometimes lift and hold and other times kneel and tend to what is underfoot. We are capable of tenderness in our parenting, pet care, and home gardening. These, too, are types of dominion.

For Jews and Christians it would seem that the most important aspect of the concept of dominion is that none of this world—nothing on land, sea, or in the air—is our own. All is gift, and all is God-given. That implies treasuring and earthkeeping. Sheep, oxen, llamas, deer, ostriches, ospreys, owls, egrets, seals, salamanders, snails, salmon, seaweed, cacti, oaks, poppies, strawberries, and banana trees are among Earth's treasures. If "dominion over" them is somehow ours, we might exercise it best if we act as gentle encouragers, nurturers, cultivators, and healers. Dominion can mean simply the support of a healthy environment. Such would seem to be the very best of biblical tradition.

Creator God, give me a power that is life energy, a power that is for flourishing and future. Give me a power that holds reverently, cultivates tenderly, and uses with elegant restraint.

For Reflection

- What concrete things am I already doing to help preserve the Earth?
- What additional one or two things can I do on behalf of some segment of the environment?

5

Danger

They lurk in secret like a lion in its covert; they lurk that they may seize the poor. **Ps 10:9**

It did not require Darwin to reveal that there is brutality and blind violence in nature. For as long as humans have been capable of noticing things, it has been evident that there are predators and prey, that what gives life to one species stills the life of another. We ourselves eat by uprooting, by picking from stalks and vines and bushes and trees, by milking, fishing, hunting, and breeding animals for slaughter. For the more genteel spirits, it can be very difficult to confront the behaviors that are part of the food chain or the aggression that is part of the human and animal instinct for survival.

Yet we are undeniably caught up in the predaciousness of nature. Sometimes we are the lion; sometimes we are the prey. To other species we humans often are what the hungry wolf is to the disabled wilderness explorer. On city streets, as well as in a solitary wilderness, we can well be the target of hungry wolves. There is a pattern here: the tendency of the stronger or the advantaged to feed on the weak. Why this should be so we simply cannot fathom. The questions of theodicy—the questions of why there should be evil and pain in a world designed by a good God—have tantalized philosophers and theologians for centuries.

Original sin hardly seems a satisfactory or full explanation for the behavior of hyenas or vicious dogs.

We might reflect on several things, however, amid the pattern of predation and food-getting. One is the fact that all of us, even vegetarians, survive on other living things. Another is the reality of our own weakness and vulnerability. Given the right set of circumstances, we can be as poor and defenseless as any small prey. Both of these realizations can lead us to gratitude: gratitude for the very fact that we do live, do survive. By our powers of reason and the good fortune of our placement on the planet, we have food, shelter, protection. We are, for the most part, surrounded with a safety net and at least the trappings of civilization. Sometimes we think to offer a grace. Rarely, however, do we consider blessing the land itself for its gifts. The bananas and bacon and breakfast cereals are not all of them; the shingles on our roofs and the locks on our windows are also part of our survival.

Yet there is another challenge to our reflection. We must confront—and it is even more imperative to do so in this age of "ecocide"—the danger we pose to all the weak and poor of any species. If we continue to contaminate and exhaust the resources of the Earth, if we continue to use without replenishing the fuels and forests and foods, if we continue to behave as though we were the only generation and the only species, we will surely imperil everyone's future.

In the psalms the lurking lion is often a symbol of bloodshed and wanton destructiveness. We are called to ask to what extent we are wreaking havoc on the defenseless of our own or any species—whether Iraqi women and children, Somalian or Sudanese infants, or Siberian tigers. We are called to the responsible admission that, because we are human and can reason, we can modify our instincts, channel our aggression, alter our patterns of food-getting, replant and reforest and restock, and set limits on what and how we consume.

While admittedly the most dangerous species on our planet, we are also the most promising—if only because we can foresee and prevent danger.

Giver of my life and sustenance, teach me gratitude and prudence. I am thankful for the lifeblood of each day and for every grain and seed and fruit that feeds me. I want to be more aware of what and how I use. Help me to be not Earth's danger but its restorer in small but significant ways.

For Reflection

- In 1989 the Ecojustice Task Force of the Presbyterian Church (U.S.A.) identified the "norms" of sustainability, participation, sufficiency, and solidarity as key to a new ecological ethics. (See *Keeping and Healing the Creation*.) The document emphasizes a future orientation as well as a present attention in our Earth efforts. It also challenges consumers to consider truly what is "sufficient" for quality of life and what is excess. In my life, what excesses might be trimmed? How can I do something concrete to offset the imbalances in consumption between First World and Third World? How am I contributing, or can I better contribute, to the well-being of other peoples and other species?

6.

Birdflight

In the Lord I take refuge; how can you say to me, "Flee like a bird to the mountains; for look, the wicked bend the bow." **Ps 11:1–2**

Even city pigeons, usually casual about human encounters, scatter from oncoming cars. Ducks blithely skimming river and lake scurry to the banks or take sudden flight at the sound of a gunshot. Every autumn over the northeast and upper midwest we can watch the orchestrated V-formation of Canadian geese winging southward before the onset of bitter winter.

These are occasional but common enough situations. However, even on the ordinary warm day, a day without traffic or gunfire or hints of Alberta clippers-to-be, we can, if we allow ourselves a measure of country and space, be eyewitnesses to the artless swing of flocks from field to trees, from lawns to bushes, from branches to bird feeders, from flower gardens to telephone lines and rooftops. We can watch the swoops and glides, the archings and lowerings of wings as birds move from shelter and rest to seed source and worm bed. Getting food and making nests set their sky paths and map their commonplace days.

Birds fly because they must. Sometimes they flee at the command of an instinct for life that drives them. Getting out of sight and out of reach is their response to hunger and cold, to bow hunter and sharpshooter.

Human flight is another story, however. We take to the airways for time-saving and professional activities more often than for adventure or exploration or the sheer pleasure of viewing the landscape from aircraft. Then again, we are more often airborne for these latter purposes than for sheer survival. The hospital "life flight," the helicopter rescue from fire or flood, the mission to drop medical supplies or food are the causes for some, though not many, of our flights.

We call the varieties of our fear responses "fight," "flight," and "freeze," and find it hard to recommend flight except when a genuine run for our lives is warranted. We tend to trivialize other types of flight and sometimes find them downright dishonorable—flights of fancy, flight to mountain hideouts or clandestine getaways. Yet we find in our human history the persistent impulse to flight—the myth of Icarus, the antics of ancients and medievals who fashioned foolhardy wings for themselves, took off and generally fell flat on their faces, the fantasies of Da Vinci. Meanwhile, we continue to crowd our skies with air traffic and to launch our probes and satellites and shuttles from Cape Kennedy. We also hang glide, parachute, and bungee jump without a twinge of regret for our ridiculousness.

Whatever our experience of or allusion to human flight, we can learn much from the habits of the birds: that there is sense in the sudden wholesale uprise to safety; that there is grace in migration to more healthful climes; that there is beauty in the reluctance to roost too long in one spot; that there is strength in the flock. There is a loveliness in the birds' nomadic quality, not just in their impulse to fly away from threat but also in the loops and turns and lightings and relocatings that are also a matter of instinct. Even the tamest pigeons and gulls and ducks don't linger overlong. We might consider our own tendencies to nest and stay. If we live on faults and flood plains, why aren't the one-time quake or inundation sufficient to warn us away? If our psyches are crumbling and our strength is sapped by conflicts and tensions that we can't hope to resolve, why don't we read the signals to seek new work and relocate? If a warmer, more hospitable, more life-sustaining region beckons, why don't we conclude that we are called to migrate? If we find a congenial, harmonious flock, why do we shy away and miss the chance that the collective beat of our wings can lift and propel us and conserve our energy?

When we are attentive, recollected, sensitive to timings, urged on to new lands and new life, better health, and more effective preservation of our young—when, that is, we are as canny as birds, we can begin to hope. If we learn humane ways to fly, we may yet awake and sing morning songs.

I seek the wisdom, God, of migrations, the good sense of when to stay and when to fly away. Give that sense not only to me but to the various flocks with which I veer. Give us grace and beauty wherever you fit us to fly.

For Reflection

- Rachel Carson entitled one of the chapters of her best-selling *Silent Spring* "And No Birds Sing." Her classic study of the deadly effects of many of the herbicides and pesticides used in the late 1950s and early 1960s sparked a generation's ecological consciousness. As she noted the disappearance of cardinals, chickadees, robins, starlings, and sparrows in the wake of heavy DDT spraying, she asked what possible value there might be in "a world without insects,…a sterile world ungraced by the curving wings of a bird in flight" (118). Why are birds important to me—for practical reasons, but also for aesthetic and spiritual ones?

7

Under Warm Wings

Guard me as the apple of the eye; hide me in the shadow of your wings.
Ps 17:8

The brooding hen, the mama bird fluffing her wings and huddling her scrawny peeps under them, is somehow like God. There is something in us, too, that needs at times to withdraw into the shade or get under cover and to rest in the watchful warmth of another. We need protective wings or protective arms to enfold us. There is surety and darkness in the shadow of motherly wings. There is quieting and the lull of a secure sleep. As the bird makes a safe home for its young, unseen forces also wait to shelter us: the omnipresence of God's love, the sustenance of human good will, the reassurance of nature's gentling, comforting features. We live, by and large, under the canopy of God's beneficence. The shadow of bird wing and the close beat of a nesting heart remind us that holding and watchful care are part of natural life and life-design, the God-design that makes for our survival.

Gather me, God, under the shelter of whatever wings I need, and help me see the many ways in which you and your world shelter me. Thank you for the brooding lives that have covered and nurtured me.

For Reflection

- Birdwatching can be fruitful even for those of us who have not adopted it as hobby or sport. What do I learn and recognize from watching birds' nesting habits?
- From the psalms' often repeated image of the "shelter" or "shadow" of God's wings, what one truth, what wisdom, about the earthly and cosmic, the human and divine, do I find being revealed?

8.

Desert Rock

And who is a rock besides our God? Ps 18:31

Anyone who has been to Sedona, Arizona, carries a memory of orange-red rock—high outcroppings amid cactus and scrub juniper and tumbleweed, cliffs the color of sunset. Their florid beauty is quite enough to evoke awe and a call to worship. Even so, there is a Chapel of the Holy Cross cut right into the Sedona cliffs, its expansive glass unstained and so providing a clear panorama of cloudless sky and sprawling desert.

There is something irresistible about the Sedona rocks, and it is something far more than the relief they provide from desert flatness. In the midst of wild heat, they are somehow cooling. They tower and cast shadow. They offer nooks, niches, crannies to crawl into. Water may even pool in their dark clefts and not be slurped up. Cactuses may indeed flower in the Sedona cliffs' glow. The urban woman can begin to see, if she pauses and lets Sedona sink into her soul, how it was that the squaws who first lived there were full and serene as they wove baskets, baked, strung beads, shaped water jars and meal bowls and wedding pottery, and bundled blankets around themselves and the young as the skies turned starstruck and darkness swallowed the heat of day. The traveler can begin to feel how steady the rock is and how it holds, at nightfall, a campfire's heat.

It is perhaps enough to notice these things.

Then, at prayer, it may be timely, too, to consider whose vestige these rocks are: One who rises up, tempers heat and chill, burnishes the landscape, widens our view and holds us, solid and still.

There is rock, great God, which I must call living. It seems to reach out and blush and breathe. Be such a rock for me.

For Reflection

- The rock of Gethsemane, the stone rolled back before the tomb of Jesus, and other rocks or stones—like the seated and reclining stone Buddhas of Polonnaruwa, Sri Lanka, which occasioned a mystical moment in the life of Thomas Merton—have achieved rich religious significance. Are there rocky places which have figured in my religious consciousness or spiritual formation? What memories, realizations, or decisions do I associate with them?

9

Deer Land

He made my feet like the feet of a deer, and set me secure on the heights.
Ps 18:33

At Ricketts Glen State Park in northeastern Pennsylvania, the rangers' cabin and information lodge at the head of the waterfalls trails through Ganoga Glen and Glen Leigh were visited one chilly autumn by a young deer the rangers had befriended. Out back there was a scattering of feed, along with the woods' own lush outlay of wild greenery, for the deer to munch. The park's pet deer had obviously been frequenting civilization's entry way and parking area since fawnhood. Along the trail that winds down the mountainside and follows the creeks through their 94-foot, 47-foot, 39-foot, 20-foot, 13-foot falls, another deer or two may, to this day, stand unflinchingly close as hikers wend their ways through the forest. These trailside deer don't get close enough to be petted, though, as the rangers' callow deer did. They exhibit no skittishness as the human trespassers in their woods happen by, but they watch at a slight remove, still and brown-eyed, pause slightly, as if to acknowledge their presence, and then resume an untroubled grazing.

We may fancy ourselves somewhat like God when we feed deer from our hands or teach them that they can stay by, assured that they are not fair game for arrows or bullets in this park. Then again, we may notice that the tamed deer somehow resemble us when we are at our most civilized, most religious, most peaceable. Perhaps so.

Or perhaps the deer are more like God. It is, after all, more their woods than ours. We are the roamers, out of our habitat. They are the rightful residents whose sleek hair blends into the bark and underbrush, whose lean forms camouflage among tall grasses and slender trees. Delicate hoof prints are their marks and traces, yet many times, like God, the deer—herds of them—remain unseen. Deer are graceful, elegant, their leaps an outstretched dance we can never even emulate, much less surpass.

Gentled, we stand and stride before all that is greater than ourselves like the young deer in the clearing at the head of the trails—soft of step, secure in our space, happily fed, confident that we are cared for. Free in the forest damp of Red Rock Mountain, the deer are as we would be: Godlike and steady. They exude harmony with the land, with waterways, with the skies unveiled in shafts through tall trees. They are at home in the universe. They never stampede us. And when we come unarmed, they can be counted on to stay quite close.

Maker of wild woodlands and glad cascades, teach us the serenity and strength of fawn and doe and buck. Lighten our footfalls and hold us calm and graced, whether we pause or leap.

For Reflection

- Given the beauty and attractiveness of deer, how do I account for the popularity and prodigality of deer hunting? Does an ethical position that considers animals as having "rights" make any sense to me? Or is there an ethic of respect which allows for seasons of hunting as well as seasons of mere deer spotting?
- Whether as totem figures in Native American religions or as Christian symbols in medieval bestiaries, deer have long been perceived as creatures with sacred meaning. What sense of the sacred might deer impart to me?

10.

Sun Revels

> In the heavens he has set a tent for the sun... Its rising is from the end of the heavens, and its circuit to the end of them; and nothing is hid from its heat. **Ps 19:4,6**

Even a sickly child in a crowded New York neighborhood learns that a chance to sit out in the sun—on the stoop or on a bench in the park— somehow is a way to feel better. The chill of staying in and staying still and the ache of bone and muscle are eased. The asthmatic finds that those spots where the sun burns away damp and mildew are places where breathing is freer. The depressed discover that moderate temperature and clear light are mood elevators, that exterior brightness is indeed vital to interior well-being. The elderly whose circulation has slowed welcome warmer days and warmer climates for the relief of stubbornly cold and stiffened hands and feet. Meanwhile, all of us, from awakening green plants and burgeoning fruit trees to brook trout and ring-necked pheasants to lowing cows and all of homo sapiens, depend on the sun as our source of life, health, energy, productivity, and good cheer. For us humans, sunlight makes for a good vacation, whether it is on Colorado ski slopes in winter, in a Pocono woodland in the fall, on a Michigan lake front in summer, or a Washington cherry blossom festival in spring. Sunshine makes our picnics and our azalea garden parties, our Volksmarch outings, our harvests and Oktoberfests.

There is a health and ease about sun. Even the most precise and skilled of photographs can never quite capture the glory and variety of the yearly round of sunstruck seasons, the daily round of sunrises and sunsets.

As earthlings, we are children of the sun. Like most of the planet's creatures, we are photo-sensitive and sun-propelled. Our living Earth has been remarkably well placed for the flourishing of life, a life that depends so fully on the star we circle, the star in whose embrace we are caught and spun.

Thus it is unfathomable that we should knowingly endanger our comradeship, our familial connection, with the sun. It boggles the mind that we should have manufactured a greenhouse effect and ozone holes that transform our life source into a peril. In this new millennium, we find that suffocating heat and ultra-violet radiation threaten us with cancers and famine. Too much sun can mean our extinction. But we have taken the Promethean vault anyway, heedlessly stealing the fire before assaying its capacity to burn.

Some of us verge on sun worship as we soak and bathe, seek spas and retire to the Sun Belt. Some of us, like Francis of Assisi, revel in the glow and the glisten, the light and warmth, the luster and shine of all creation, and write or sing or dance or pray or paint our canticles to the sun. We see the sun as a sign of God. But, perversely, madly, maddeningly, we proceed to douse its benefit and kill ourselves with our chemicals, our smoke, our craving for capital.

God, give me a love for the gold of your gift, the life-giving, healing sun. And give me a holy dread of the gold that is mammon, the greed that turns sun's fire deadly for us. Let us revel in the sun as given and restrain our artifices and technological machinations.

For Reflection

- Solstices and equinoxes can spark celebrations and hosannas. In what simple ways do I celebrate the gift of seasons and of changes in time and the length of sunlight? How does my church mark the change of seasons?
- The human relationship with the sun can be an ambiguous one, since the sun can be both life-giving and death dealing. When have I experienced the ambiguity of the sun's effect? How have I learned to live with reverence for its power?

11.

The Human Heart

May God grant you your heart's desire, and fulfill all your plans. **Ps 20:4**

What does the human heart want? Nutrients, oxygen, and exercise certainly, but also so very much more. We so want tenderness, for example, that we call certain events, stories, films, and encounters "heartwarming." We so long for stimulation that we prize the episodes—whether they are athletic feats or romantic interludes or intellectual stimuli or sensory thrills—that "set our hearts beating faster." We feel alive when the thump in our chest strengthens or quickens; we bask and glow when our hearts are slowed or calmed in a long, lingering, loving moment; we are encouraged upon the arrival of unexpected good news. Such moments are "heartening." What we want, then, is not only life itself but also a life that is full. We want love, friendship, and relaxation. We long for at-homeness and ease. We also want challenge, success, beauty, surprise, and a general newness of things.

An old dictum about the popularity of iambic pentameter (the rhythmic line favored by Shakespeare) is that it imitates the rhythm of heartbeat (lubbDUPP) and breath (a 5:1 ratio). A homespun observation of young pups is that they can sleep alone in their doggie baskets if an alarm clock has been wrapped in a blanket and set there to tick as if it is their mother's heart. For us humans too, there is a secure intimacy in our hearing or our remembering a close heartbeat.

The human heart has become the symbol for courage and love. For Catholics, devotion to the Sacred Heart of Jesus has evoked an awareness of divine compassion. The hearts of Jesus and Mary appear as religious images for unconditional love, sacrifice, and endurance of pain and sorrow.

Life sign, love token: the heart is that mighty muscle which we humans share metaphorically with deity and materially with a variegated assemblage of species of the animal kingdom. The heart seems to be as much the core of our visions and projects as it is the source of our pulses.

Perhaps because it is so much a symbol of life and love, the heart also has ready associations with our vulnerability. Our personal dramas can be heartrending, and we are subject not only to physical heart attack but also to emotional heartache and heartbreak. Deep disappointment can leave us heartsick. We can be assailed by life and, as a result, lose heart. We witness acts of cruelty or utter apathy and deem them heartless. So, amid the regular and steady thump, the human heart can also remind us, by our very language, of fragility, bereftness, and sudden arrest.

The heart provides idioms of strong feeling. It floods and ebbs as the great tides of our affections and anxieties wash in and out. All the while we continue to beat and breathe in the heart of the world and to cast our cares and hopes upon the heart of God. That heart, in the midst of things, may be all that we, in the heart of this world, finally want: the Heart of hearts.

God, there is a wonder of chambers and blood and of pulsing flesh that I seldom notice. Yet the image of heart adorns my speech and the décor around me. Let me enter deeply into the wonder of the human heart and render heartfelt thanks.

For Reflection

- The prayer of St. Augustine is well known: "You have made us for yourself, O God, and our hearts are restless until they rest in you." What restlessness of life and heart do I contend with?
- When am I most attuned to the beating of a heart? Do I pause to give thanks for that life gift?

12.

The Dust of Death

To him, indeed, shall all who sleep in the earth bow down; before him shall bow all who go down to the dust, and I shall live for him. **Ps 22:29**

"Like plants, our bodies remain vulnerable to injury and decay. Like animals," Harold Kushner observes, "we can grow sick and die" (*When Bad Things Happen to Good People*, 66). Furthermore, "it is one thing to explain that mortality in general is good for people in general," he notes. "It is something else again to tell someone who has lost a parent, a wife, or a child, that death is good" (Kushner, 71).

Death is natural, the rabbi reminds us, and even good. It is good in the sense that it assures the Earth of diversity, multiplicity, and transformations in its species. It is also motivating for humans in the sense that a consciousness of our mortality forces us to do, to produce, to improve, and to promote change with full knowledge that we cannot procrastinate on into infinity. Our earthly lives are framed by birth and death. In solidarity with all living things, we must and will go down into the dust. Our uniqueness lies in the fact that we know this. Declining and dying is as natural as the turning of the Earth and the shift from blossom to green leaf to burnt orange to bare limb. So we feel the pressure to do and make beautiful things and to finish what we have begun. However, we also mourn.

Some of us, like a good-humored octogenarian in a Philadelphia parish, may joke with our friends that we repeatedly tell God, "Don't call me yet. I'll let you know when I'm ready!" Some of us, like her, are still having fun and want to live through and beyond the next dance. Some of us cope with the reality of our own deaths with the Scarlett O'Hara coping mechanism: resolve to think about it tomorrow. Some of us grieve the dead we've loved and known by memorializing them in picture albums and anniversary masses. Others of us deal with deaths by going silent and numb. All things considered, even in rugged times, we cling to life. We miss the living persons who have lit our days with their wisdom and laughter. And we grieve the passing of favored countryside vistas, of trees that cooled our youthful summers, pets that comforted us with their familiarity, their loyalty, and their soft selves.

How, then, ought we to look at death? Faith in an afterlife, anticipation of reunion with beloved relatives and friends in heaven, and hope for bliss in the beatific vision can certainly help. So too can the promise of some sort of new creation, the resurrection of the body, some manner of "new earth" and "new heavens" such as Scripture foretells. But we might also think of our lastingness in a more practical and more immediately earthly sense. When the life breath leaves us, we return to the Earth that has nurtured us. We return to the cosmic dust that shaped the atoms and molecules of our skin and hair and blood and bone. We break down again to something of the starstuff from which we were built up. And we somehow become part of what lives beyond us—the soil itself, the plants and trees that spring up, the animals and humans who feed on whatever of us has seeped back through the Earth. We also live in the cells and pathways of human memory and are transformed there into values and gladnesses and realizations and second thoughts that are passed on.

Having come from "mother Earth" we mother future generations with what is left of our ideas, our flesh, and our breath.

In a number of ways, then, we do indeed live on, which seems all the more reason to live fully and freely while we do still live, and all the more reason to live the present beyond the present's pain. This means to live, not only in hope but in the confidence that in every moment we are somehow more than we are aware we are. We carry with us the lives

35

of everyone and everything we have loved, and our love is among the material and immaterial things we pass on.

God whom I worship, God of life, give me the breadth and the spirit to live, really and richly, until I die. Fix my vision on the life that outlasts pain and makes new life from the dust of death.

For Reflection

- Psalm 22, despite its exultant climax (rendered "And to him my soul shall live" in the New American Bible translation), is an outcry of physical pain and psychic torment. How do I deal with, or find meaning in, prolonged pain?
- What would I consider a gentle death, a good death?

13.

Sheep Pasturing

The Lord is my shepherd, I shall not want. He makes me lie down in green pastures; he leads me beside still waters; he restores my soul. **Ps 23:1–3**

The village of Stillwater, Pennsylvania, is a rural spot where corn grows, cows graze, and sheep pasture on grassy hills. Thick and taut under their close tufts of wool, the sheep mosey and leave the stains of hoof prints on the low-munched plots. Fishing Creek streams slowly by, and two old wooden covered bridges have become a minor tourist attraction of the region.

The best days in Stillwater are glistening autumn days with glints of orange, yellow, red, and fading green flagging from the trees; days when diamonds seem to dance on the surface of the stream and disappear as soon as the wader would grasp them; days when brook trout and min-nows galore, a surprising heron, and the reliable ducks are still warm enough to swish and stay.

Who knows where the birds or the mulling sheep disappear to when the creek glazes over with inches of ice and the hardwood trees are nipped with frost and a season of snow is slathered over the hills? Whatever mud might be is frozen, and farmers' and children's long johns and tall socks flap and then stiffen on the last clotheslines in

America. Somewhere south the birds find greenery, we guess, and sun and food. Someone in barns or under shelters tends the sheep. When the first hint of warmth appears, or even the momentary thaw, they reappear. Then spring comes and summer, and lambs wobble and lean their way uphill and grow fuzzy. Bleats strengthen and deepen and resound across low mountains as robin and starling and grackle and bluejay and finch fests ensue.

It is not too hard to say why we humans have been more content to think of ourselves as sheep than, let's say, cows or goats. It seems to have something to do with the fact that we have so long imagined God better as shepherd than as cowboy or farmer or goatherd. That, of course, has everything to do with the terrain and conventions of Israel. From the psalmist to Ezekiel to Jesus, we see ourselves with God and before God as sheep to shepherd. We are free, in some sense, to wonder and wander in the goodness of the Earth. We have all day to graze in its bright glints. We grow, to a certain extent, our own warmth. Yet we are made secure when we sense the watchful nearness of a rescuer, a gatherer, a guide, a God whose panorama is wider than our own. We are relieved to think of that God as providence and safe haven—knowing, as we do so well, that there are stern limits to our ability to provide for ourselves and that there are rickety foundations to many of our havens. We need someone to call us into lasting warmth and calm from the inevitable cycles of snowstorm.

The rural Pennsylvania sheep are not pure romance and fleece. They make noise and get grubby. They can swipe the grass from the land to its very roots. But they live in peace. And they have enough of themselves to be shorn and reshorn and reshorn so that others (we) need not be bitten by winter's chill. They pasture under the care of a God they can neither know nor name.

We, meanwhile, have more than an instinct that there is a watchful herder yonder yet near, letting us be, yet grasping prod and crook. We relax in the thought that we can surrender ourselves, as sheep do, to pasturing, flocking, shearing amid beauty, by still waters, encircled by the certainties of Earth and sky.

Shepherd me, God, as you have done and do. I rest in your care and thank you for the many provident gifts that keep me. Cast your kindly glance and extend a guiding hand over all your flock, in all seasons.

For Reflection

- Psalm 23 is probably the most popular of the psalms, used as it is for comfort in calm seasons, in times of sickness, and at funeral liturgies. When has it been most meaningful to me? Which images or associations from this psalm resound most strongly with me?
- Shepherds figured daily in the lives of the children of Israel in whose time the psalms were written. If the psalms were being written today, would there be any persons who might remind many of us of God in the same way? To what creatures other than sheep might we compare ourselves?

14.

The Whole Earth

The earth is the Lord's and all that is in it, the world and those who live in it. **Ps 24:1**

During the whoosh of morning traffic on the parkways, it may be difficult to detect that, even in a season of pumpkins and gourds and Indian
corn, there are still berry trees bearing and geraniums blooming in
small plots of downtown Pittsburgh. In the whirr and signaling of fax
messages, computer printouts, and digital watch beeps, it is easy to miss
the honks of Canadian geese. Every now and then an enterprise arises
that reminds us that there is a vast world beyond all that is manufactured, made-in-the-USA. After a massive vetch planting purpled and
then over-purpled the summer landscape, wildflower gardens appeared
along Pennsylvania interstates. Projects like these, along with the state
parks and county nature preserves and bird sanctuaries we establish, do
their best to make space for many species' flourishing and to retain
habitats. Public television airs "Wild America," and specials from
National Geographic periodically break across the networks. All of this
somehow reminds us that elephant trumpets and trumpet vines are in
our midst and are not of our making, that chicory and chickadees rise
up without our willing them.

All the Earth, beyond our concrete and asphalt and brick and artifice, is in some sense a cornucopia of life. Kelp and fish, seas and streams, dune grass and laurel, Sequoias and coral, peacocks and palmettos, aardvarks and bobcats, dolphins and avocados, Ethiopians and Eskimos splay and color our landscape. Some of us believe that the minerals and rocks too are alive—the granite and quartz, the turquoise and emerald, the limestone and shale. The Earth itself would be as much botanical garden, arboretum, zoo, aviary, aquarium, or canyon pueblo as anyone would need were it not for our eye-fix on license plates, computer monitors, antennae, and airport control towers.

Caught as we are in expressway snarls and boulevard jug handles and fiber optic tangles and e-mail overload, we tend not to think of gnats and lily pads as some of the ways in which God loves us. Nor are we likely to think of salmon runs or the frowsy scatter of dandelion heads as the way the world loves God. Yet all the nature mystics would say that this is precisely how love works. The breath of God awakens something simple and unusual—a Galapagos turtle, let's say, or a tiger lily, or a Filipino woman with a genius for piano. And every being awakened by God—since every being is simple and unusual—loves back by being itself. Mystics never cease to remark upon this. The only reason the rest of us aren't mystics is that we let ourselves get distracted on the way to noticing love.

On the other hand, the fact that we invent and technologize is an expression of our being what and who we are. It becomes problematic, though, when we forget our sources—God and the good Earth—and begin to imagine that we and our artificial brainchildren are the whole of the universe. Our being sickens when we forget to see and breathe. There are, by the way, palm trees in Rome, grasshoppers in New York, raccoons on Pittsburgh's north side, heron rookeries just outside Detroit, gulls over the rivers and lake and dunes around Chicago, saguaro and all sorts of other cacti in Phoenix, cows and thickets of ivy and vine in the Moraga Valley just outside San Francisco and Oakland. Anyone can see them. There are also seventeen types of wildflower on a very small plot of land on a mountain summit near Scranton. Who knows what might reside in and around all the cities where some of us have never landed. There are, too, people everywhere, some of whom smile and give thanks as they see and breathe.

I behold everywhere a kaleidoscope of earthly things! Thank you, extravagant God, for the splendor of creation. Help me be the beauty you have crafted me to be, and help me let all the life around me be.

For Reflection

- Each January, Worldwatch prints its State of the World report, alerting us to environmental issues and concerns: topsoil depletion, variables in crop production, over-fishing, endangered species, water and air pollution, population challenges. What ecological issue most presses me? What have I done or am I doing to promote biodiversity?
- What creaturely beauty (nonhuman or human) have I recently discovered and come to admire?

15.

Thunderings

The voice of the Lord is over the waters; the God of glory thunders. **Ps 29:3**

No storm in the Pennsylvania mountains can ever be quite like a thunderstorm rolling across Lake Michigan into Whiting and Hammond, Indiana, and then on across the Indiana prairies. Thunder that bangs back and forth in valleys is also somehow muted and ingested by the mountains, dissipated in banks of fir and spruce and pine leaves, slowed in the dip of ravines. But the lakeshore storm just clamors overhead, and the thunderous booms descend unmuffled. There is nothing for them to fall into but rooftops, warehouses, an oil refinery, and an endless expanse of flat land. Storms roll relentlessly and long.

If one were pressed to choose which of these types of thunderstorms one would prefer, the choice would not be too easy. The mountain storm seems somehow softer, the lightning path more mysterious. It is hard to say how much of the storm is happening on the other side of the mountain or a valley away. The lakeshore storm is more violent but also more direct. One can trace the lightning spear quite straight with unobstructed view. One gets the full force of thunderslap and somehow comes to know it more intimately. The mountain storm is a long rumble, and one never knows for sure where it is coming from. The lakeshore blitz is here and now, overhead without doubt, and all across a lake that seems as large as an ocean.

God, we might conjecture, could be like either. A trifle suppressed, a bit less trackable, locatable by clues (like spotting the lightning shoot and then counting 1001, 1002, 1003 to judge how many miles away the center of the storm might be): a God in hiding, *Deus absconditus*, a God of hints and echoes who needs to be pursued and who expects our hit-and-miss. Such might be the thundering "God of glory." But God might also be entirely too obvious, banging over our heads, around our ears, setting the Earth vibrating under our feet, leaving us nowhere to run to, no cover to duck in: a God who overwhelms, an inescapable God, a God who is too much for us, all around and straight up, *mysterium tremendum*.

God is sometimes the mountain storm, sometimes the lakeside cannonade and downpour. Either gets our attention and helps us to welcome the more steady, reliable frequent God: the God of clear skies and calm.

God of battering and flash, perk me to your presence. Signal me so that I hear, close up or faraway, your might, your resonance, and your glory.

For Reflection

- Aside from storms, what other manifestations of nature suggest to me God's glory and God's mystery?
- Among the familiar miracle stories of the gospels is that of Jesus calming the storm at sea. When I consider the storms I have encountered, whether literal storms or psycho-spiritual storms, can I recognize how God has been present in the storm? Can I also see how God has been very active amid every calm?

16.

❧❦❧

Mountain Magnificence

By your favor, O Lord, you had established me as a strong mountain. **Ps 30:7**

Traffic reporters have a heydey with speculations about what the first spraying of highway salt means for the newly bought or newly painted auto. When snowfall comes early, the pockmarks of rock salt are perhaps all that some may notice. However, the traveler crossing the summits of the Allegheny mountains (where the signmakers announce: "Highest Point on I-80 East of the Mississippi") cannot help but be overcome with a sense of "winter wonderland." The evergreen boughs are coated with white and glisten as the morning sun rises and rises. The slopes down to the low valleys are sugared, and the sure brown of bark and the steady reds and whites of farmhouses and the dark weatherboard of barns stand out. The smoke-curls match cloud and snow-blow and are one with them.

To be a mountain in the first few inches of late autumn or early winter snow is majestic. Even more majestic, some might say, is to be a mountain when the first blossoms and sprigs of green appear after a long season of barbed, leafless trees and snow that has gone gray and gravelly. More beauteous still, perhaps, is the summer mountain lush with green-leaf, ivy, laurel, wild grass, fern, and a rainbow of berries and wildflowers. Yet there is still the autumn flare of yellow, orange, brown, red, darkening

45

green, and the flutter of leaves gone airborne till mountains go, weeks later, to a sleep of steel bark and foliage the color of wilt and rust. What can be more glorious than a mountain in the temperate zone where snow cover goes to bud, and bud goes to blooming, and bloom goes to blaze, and blaze goes to die-down, where it waits again for a blanket of snow? To be such a mountain would be to spin and flaunt and furl and settle, knowing all the while that each season is incomparable, each peak is somehow unsurpassable, and beauty will be born in warmth or chill.

The psalmist whose self seemed like a mountain celebrated the new day's joy after night darkness, and hailed the turn from "mourning into dancing" (Ps 30:11). The mountain that goes resplendent when winter, spring, summer, fall unveil and burst, begin, and climax also stands under mornings of fog, days of downpour, overnights of blizzard, weeks of drought, and months of ice. What the watcher sees and photographs or paints or imprints in memory or tells are the mountain scenes that break through long waits.

There is, the mountains seem to say, the championship moment, the masterpiece day. When those come, all drabbery and dullness drift into oblivion and seem to matter little. The inner power of color and change overcome everything else, and there is simply awe.

God of variegation and mountain glow, show me that I and all creatures go through dormancies and yet in great moments blaze forth. As the seasons of life turn, ready me for many glistenings, blossomings, flowerings and flarings. Give me gentle rest and good faith on the days of frost and fade.

For Reflection

- Aldo Leopold, in a classic environmental note, suggested that "thinking like a mountain" invites us to a new sense of awareness and a new humility about the inner workings and interweavings of things. When have I thought like a mountain? What have I summoned to my consciousness at such times?
- What mountain moments have inspired the response of awe from me? What mountain moments might evoke patience?

17.

Sun Time

My times are in your hand...Let your face shine upon your servant; save me in your steadfast love. **Ps 31:15–16**

In the hunt-and-gather days, in the era of candles and lanterns at home and on the farm, in all the stretch of centuries before gaslight and electricity, we knew what daylight meant. It was time to work with our hands, arrange things, and travel from town to town. When dusk set in and lengthened into all the dark hours till dawn, we told stories, sang, rested by fire or stove, and slept. We understood that without light there was nothing to do but huddle close, picture what we remembered and imagined in rhythms and words, settle down, and snooze. Sunup meant awakening to birdsong and having light enough to roam and do. Only the insects chattered all night.

To think of God as the shining day meant, for the psalm-singers, to ascribe to God the qualities of warmth and illumination, the qualities that allowed for horizon scan, exploration, provision-getting, and intricate activity. It also implied that slowing down and sitting still and dozing off when light faded were part of the divine order of things. For all people then knew, God went somewhere else when the sun sank behind the hills or into the ocean. Perhaps God too napped while they did.

There was time to run and time to stop, time to work and time to watch, all ordered by the risings and settings of the sun.

In our time the cycle of workday and ease has yielded to round-the-clock shifts and all-night restaurants, grocery stores, video rentals, television programming, satellite linkups, fax messages, ceaseless e-mail, blue or green print scurrying across screens. For corporate life and even for personal life, "24-7" is set forth as a goal, as the optimum: humanity in perpetual motion. When we think of God at all, we might vaguely summon up notions of kindliness, generosity, inspiration, omnipresence, pleasant surprise. In a society structured around endless workdays, we like to think of God as gentle interlude and all-around nice guy. However, we are forgetful of the God of the Sabbath, of Sundays.

Once upon a time God ordained a weekly day of rest. Once upon a time the hours of darkness called a halt to each day's activities. The author of Ecclesiastes sat staring at night into a fire and knew that all the day's labor could be "a chasing after wind" (Eccl 1:14). The psalmist knew that the length of days could be battle and that the only way that made sense of things and delivered us was walking in Godlight. They learned these things because they observed sun time. They remembered that sun gave energy, strength, and sight for doing and doing. But they noticed, too, that night invited contemplation and called much doing into question. It was time for listening and laughter but also for serious thought and serious talk. It was time to "wait for the Lord" attentively (v. 24). The biblical authors, like all in their day, knew the obvious that we have nearly lost: that the sun comes up and out by itself, after all the dark; that dark is the time to settle back, reconsider, recoup. After the respite of night and dreaming, sun time is the time for us again to skip and spark.

God, restore to me the cycles of light and quiet. Attune me again to sun time, to rhythms of activity and rest. Still in me whatever it is—pride or overdrive— that would hurtle through days nonstop, in artificial light.

For Reflection

- Over the past decade, an increasing number of studies have suggested that Americans, for the most part, suffer from sleep deprivation. Why is it that I tend to neglect my own urge for physical and mental rest? How do I succumb to societal pressure by lengthening my days, shortening my nights, structuring a life with longer and longer hours of work? Do I genuinely observe any Sabbaths?

- Josef Pieper, in a book entitled *Leisure: The Basis of Culture*, suggested that times of restfulness and non-productivity are actually the most likely to be productive of the arts, conversation, and imaginative leaps. How much time do I allow for cultural activities and creative thoughts?

18.

Sea Water

He gathered the waters of the sea as in a bottle; he put the deeps in storehouses. **Ps 33:7**

The child who discovers ocean in Sea Isle City, New Jersey, or at Folly Beach outside Charleston, South Carolina, can hardly begin to fathom—even as her mind asks—what basin or tub could be big enough to hold all that water. The adult beachcomber often forgets to ask, accepting the fact of ocean, and unless she is an oceanographer, she won't worry a trifle about how deep it really is at Mindanao or what occurs when there's a submarine volcano. Only a mind larger than the Earth could really quite grasp the magnitude of sea space. Certainly only a vision wider than ours, and only a far more artful hand, could fashion such a thing as ocean.

Largeness is too much for us. Containing expansiveness—of water or of thought—requires even greater expansiveness: channels in, rivulets out, release mechanisms like evaporation and flood. Oceanic thoughts, like oceans themselves, demand some boundary as well as some expression. Only divine design and divine mind would seem able to set these limits and to determine what shores might be broken on.

No mortal can encompass ocean. No ocean can exceed the Earth. And human thought can descend only so far, fill only so full, break upon only so much shore. Wherever we turn, whether outward to sea or inward to the recesses of mind and soul, we can hardly help but begin to notice that we cannot stretch and reach as far as God.

We can, however, discover awe.

God, you are greater than our imaginings and wiser in your works than we can even grasp. Help me see and stand in wonder before the many offerings and phenomena of Earth that are beyond my comprehension.

For Reflection

- There is a certain human fascination with submarine travel, the study of undersea life, diving deep as well as summering at seashores and combing the beaches for shells and treasure. How do I explain the special attraction the ocean holds for me?
- In a lifetime one can experience many oceanic thoughts and oceanic feelings. What have been some of mine?

19.

Ravenous Lions

The young lions suffer want and hunger, but those who seek the Lord lack no good thing.
Ps 34:10

New stories and video footage of drought and famine have become all too familiar in recent decades. Americans have seen starvation in Africa and have been frustrated by warlords and the maneuverings of local politicos as food has been used to bribe and barter. Less frequently the scenes of starving animals have been shown too—carcasses rotting under the desert sun or ghostly four-legged forms of hide wrapped thinly over bone on their last prowl for food and water. We have seen such scenes even in the American west.

We learn that, for humans and for animals, when hunger becomes prolonged, it first crazes. We will kill what we would usually leave in peace if the pangs and cramps are severe enough. When hunger goes on even longer, however, it dulls and deadens. There is a hunger so extreme that even the will to eat ceases, and the strength to lift even a morsel to the mouth is sapped. A numb motionlessness sets in, and then a slow death.

The starving young lion is poignant. The monarch of beasts at what would ordinarily be the coming-to-be of agility, speed, and muscular strength prowls pathetically around the edges of dried-up water holes and watches for anything that moves close enough so as not to require more than a quick swoop. An emaciated gazelle hardly makes a worthwhile meal. The energy required for a capture may surpass the energy provided by the meat of the prey. The once mighty lion is left to shamble about nuzzling the dry, grassless land hoping a last hope that some mangy things might happen along to be easily slashed and eaten. Meanwhile dust devils swirl around, and the sun beats on.

The want that turns to wildness and eventually goes numb has been observed, to some extent, in every human need and in every visible species. The thirty-fourth psalm does not speak of the ache and hunger caused by calamities of nature, however. Providential design does not ordinarily interrupt or prevent such things. The psalm speaks instead, it seems, of hunger that might be prevented, hunger brought on. There are bodily hungers for humans and for animals that better planning and wiser use of resources might have forestalled. Then too, there are hungers of the heart, hungers of mind, hungers of the soul that can be fed if we are canny and attentive. The presence of the Lord, the psalmist suggests, is watersource and feeding ground that never dries up. It is seedbed of the better idea, the humane response, the foresight that can meet gaunt need. God never desires maddened waste. God never thins out to uselessness, never shrivels up into taut carcass or lifeless tuft of pale, burnt grass and weed. The starvation of humans and animals in a rainless land is tragedy, and some of what others can do is to offer relief and attempt to spare additional lives. Starvation for love, for knowledge, for the spirit world is, however, the worst of senselessness. It would be as if the lion starved because it simply chose not to move, flex muscle, or chew while food was at its very feet. Or as if someone caged the lion just far enough away to prevent it from getting any food. Ignoring animal and human want is perversity, godlessness. Godlessness is a kind of anorexic disdain for what is most needed just to live.

God, you do not will, I know, the famine and want that leads to death. Make all of us wiser and more prudent in our responses to the starvation of the world's poor, the world's children, the world's herds and flocks. Help me, too, to be attuned to the starvation of spirit and to offer you fitting food.

For Reflection

- Forecasts for our twenty-first century have suggested that famine and drought will likely beset more and more populous lands. What means have I undertaken to address world hunger?
- What hungers have I encountered recently in people whom I have met in work or ministry?

20.

Kinship

You save humans and animals alike, O Lord. Ps 36:6

Jeffrey Moussaieff Masson and Susan McCarthy demonstrate, by anecdote after anecdote in *When Elephants Weep*, that animals can grieve, hold grudges, comfort, adopt, tease, torture, endanger themselves for the benefit of another, be lonely and depressed, rejoice, play, and even sometimes keep a pet. What Masson and McCarthy suggest is that animals may indeed have rich inner lives that humans barely detect. From the dwarf mongoose to the chimpanzee, from the otter to the orca, from the macaw to the elephant, a variety of animals rally, form allegiances, care for their own kin and others, communicate, and exhibit traits of "personality"—shyness, generosity, timidity, trust. Frans de Waal claims, in "Chimpanzee Justice," that primates can and do develop patterns of law enforcement, punishment, restitution, and reconciliation. A number of primates have developed vocabularies in American Sign Language, and both chimpanzees and elephants have learned to draw and paint, note Masson and McCarthy.

What all this suggests is that humans ought to tread lightly on the ground that holds animals to be mere brutes—tools, foodstuff, amusement, exhibit, hunting prey, and trophy. It seems increasingly clear that they cannot exist merely for us. Their lives have quality. Much about animals urges us to regard them as ends-in-themselves, creatures with their own reason for being, their own internal value, their own social structure.

Claims that elephants weep and lemurs make friends may seem the matter for fables and Disney fantasies. Yet the fact that a number of naturalists and ethicists have been persuaded that animals do indeed have interior lives—emotional lives, affinities for beauty, and behaviors that seem worshipful, religious—urges us humans to acknowledge them as more than simply ours.

Our own human religious impulse can and ought to move us to some honoring of animals as kin. While often useful, interesting, and companionable to us, animals are ultimately not our own. They have their own destinies. They belong to God, who may indeed find them not only pleasurable but full of their own meaning. The more that we learn, the less we may find them unlike us.

God of my family, God of my kin, help me be mindful of your steadfast love for all and your desire for our flourishing together.

For Reflection

- A host of writers on "animal rights" and "animal respect" have produced books on human obligations to animals. The World Wildlife Fund and PETA have varied approaches to concern for animals. Do I see animals as bearing "rights"? If so, what rights and with what limits? If not, do I concede that humans owe animals respect? In what ways? With what constraints on human behavior?

21.

Things Passing

Do not fret because of the wicked; do not be envious of wrongdoers, for they will soon fade like the grass, and wither like the green herb. **Ps 37:1–2**

As cold and wind set in, the cornfield and the vegetable garden go stiff, anemic, scrawny. Lithe greenery turns to snapping twig, and brown old leaves go down to mulch. Soon snow covers over an anonymous pile of rotting stuff, and everyone heads to storehouses or south for eating. In the temperate zones, the land lies still as hibernation, and the point comes at which dried herbs lose the last of their scent.

Such drying up comes with winter or with drought. Winter, at least, has its measures in the rhythm of seasons and holds within it the promise of spring. Drought, however, looks like the death of everything. Crops go down to stubble, the sweat of planting yields nothing to reap, and acres where humus should be cake the landscape with dust whenever breezes blow.

Both are natural, the winter withering and the drought death. And both may reveal something of the end to which evildoing comes. Evildoing, post-lapsarians believe, is not natural. On the other hand, it seems quite so, since it is all of human history that we know. What it comes to varies, though. There is a wintry evil that chills and saps but somehow, down a ways, leaves soil fertile enough for something green and new and good to grow. It is the battlefield that becomes a park, the criminal soul that turns evangelical. But there is the drought evil, too, the evil that stunts growth and starves people. Bellies of children distend, flies gather around faces, and the bones of slow death are left in new deserts. It is almost impossible to coax any good from such evil—except, perhaps, the eked-out lesson, the resolution to learn and prevent.

God of the turnabout, give us light to learn from the disasters of our human actions and the will to plant and water anew.

For Reflection

- We can chant litanies of the sites of latter twentieth-century environmental disasters: Miamata, Love Canal, Chernobyl, Bhopal, Prince William Sound, burning Iraqi oilwells. And we can catalog the wild weathers and the eerie warmth of the early twenty-first century as the wages of eco-sin. What am I doing to redress wrongs against persons and the Earth in which I might have played some small part?

22.

Inheritors of the Land

But the meek shall inherit the land, and delight themselves in abundant prosperity. Ps 37:11

It is the promise of a psalm, echoed five times over. It is a proclamation of beatitude. The have-nots shall have. The poor shall be flush with wealth.

It is the dangerous threat of the Magnificat. The mighty shall tumble from their thrones. The rich shall feel the gnaw of hunger in their guts. The reckless and greedy, the bullies and tyrants, will see their power crumble and their successes end in slop.

If our justice and our generosity were like God's, no one would have to mention these things.

Attune me, God, to your sense of right, wealth, flourishing. And help me reorder my life, especially my use of things, for the good of all. Make me meek where I should be.

For Reflection

- Low enforcement of environmental laws, dumps for hazardous wastes, reluctance to clean up water and soil are everyday occurrences in areas where the population of the poor is high. What can we do to alter this picture?
- What advantages in eating, heating, cooling, housing, accessing medical care, learning, working, traveling, and playing do I enjoy that billions do not? What would I be willing to let go of in order to share more equitably?

23.

The Depths

Deep calls to deep at the thunder of your cataracts; all your waves and your billows have gone over me. **Ps 42:7**

There are times of drenching and times of desperation. There are times when pulse and pace are slowed and depressed at the thought of a past world, a lost time, a broken dream, a shattered love, a haze ahead. God may seem sleeping, dead, or a slithering mirage. Our force and drive seem as drained away as blood from a fatal wound.

On days when the skies are gone military gray, drizzle falls steadily on the Canadian side of Niagara Falls. The incautious—those without parkas or raincoats—are caught unawares, and the half prepared find their umbrellas ineffective against a sideways spray. The downhearted can see where the force of the falls has bored holes in rock and note how pools too sudden and deep to be measured can be formed by a rushing liquid wear-away.

Yet there is a strange pleasure to that rain and the mighty gush of river that falls over the Niagara ledges. The awestruck ride the Maid of the Mist. The curious explore the Castle of the Wind. The roar of water overpowers human voice, birdcall, and bell sound. The roll of the Niagara over wild rock reminds us that rivers last, as do rocky beds and cliffs and startling downpours and spume that dampens flesh.

Even on a day gone charcoal, there is an assurance to the river. Time flashes and waits—tons of water a second, centuries to change a contour.

When one sees the plaques that mark the "discovery" of the Niagara by the European, when one sees the photos made not long after photography was invented, when one thinks of Iroquois, Mohawk, or whoever happened by, and the bears and the evergreens and the squirrels and the wild grass that came long before, one can only think of endurance. Endurance.

Underneath it all, is "steadfast love." A wide river, a drop of rock, a shape to a landscape. A place to stop, be saturated, and remember that things last mysteriously, far beyond human span and ken.

God of the long waterfall, awaken my heart with hope, with a sense of time beyond time. You who are steadfast love, let me endure in love for so many enduring things.

For Reflection

- A first look, and even a second, at the Niagara can be totally startling. What is it about natural wonders that attracts and enlarges me?
- When or where have I allowed a close encounter with a waterfall or water-force to shift my perception of space, time, and meaning?

24.

Living Earth

We will not fear, though the earth should change, though the mountains shake in the heart of the sea; though its waters roar and foam, though the mountains tremble with its tumult. **Ps 46:2–3**

In the late 1970s British chemist and cyberneticist James Lovelock presented to the public his Gaia hypothesis: the idea that the Earth as a whole may be thought of as a single (though highly complex) organism, a "living entity." Using the ancient Greek name for Mother Earth—a name that was not merely a personification but an expression of a conviction that the Earth itself was an energetic living being, Lovelock proposed that the Earth has within it remarkable self-sustaining qualities, capacities for adjusting and balancing organic and inorganic systems such that conditions for life are maintained. Lovelock's Gaia hypothesis suggests that the Earth as a whole has within it an energetic self-regulating system that is comparable to the human body's homeostasis. Only when under drastic assault from infection, neglect, traumatic injury, or the like does human homeostasis break down. Similarly, Lovelock's hypothesis or "model," as he calls it, surmises that the Earth has remarkable resilience, an ability to adjust and readjust as weather, geological phenomena, and behaviors of organisms shift. As with the human organism, extraordinary stresses may sometimes have disabling effects on the organism, Earth. For the most part, though, the planet can keep its balance. Atmospheric gases, salinity of oceans, global conditions for organic flourishing, even while perhaps impaired in certain areas, persist and prevail.

The Lovelock model and the evidence for it are persuasive. As such, the Gaia hypothesis occasions a certain confidence and serenity. It suggests that Earth itself can withstand a certain amount of cataclysm and battering. It even hints that what humans experience as disasters and flukes may in fact be part of the living Earth's self-correcting mechanism. Processes larger than ourselves are at work, Lovelock reminds us.

What is perhaps most needed on an ethical level is the development of our ability to apply scientific knowledge to our human patterns of habitat selection, so-called "development," sites for agriculture, fishing, lumbering, and industry. We must wonder about the wisdom of settling on flood plains, the San Andreas fault, or the shadowlands beneath potentially reactivated volcanoes. Furthermore, we need to challenge ourselves to enact policies to prevent our human technologies from levying assaults on the atmosphere, the waters, the land, and living species assaults that can impair and disable "Gaia."

"Be still and know that I am God," this psalm adjures and admonishes (v 10). What is most needed on the spiritual level is not a revival of goddess worship and dedications to Gaia but a reverence for all that lives, all that has been conceived by the Source of life. In the midst of stress and strife, the psalmist says, it is needful to withdraw to some space from which we can see a broader panorama. We need to recognize that the present upset, quake, eruption, or storm, may be part of a larger healing or revivifying process.

For those who believe in a Creator God while also giving credence to scientific accounts of global evolution and transformation, the Gaia hypothesis can be a source of comfort: a reassurance that the Earth moves and shifts in order to awaken, restore its energies, and adapt to new conditions for life. However, it can also be an admonition that the life source for the living Gaia is an enlivening, creative God who calls us to cooperation and preservation. "The God of life" is what Gustavo Gutierrez calls God: the God who moves all beings toward fullness of life and resists those who thwart life.

Awaken me, God, to the way in which local storms and stresses (even the storms and stresses in my own heart) and the larger climatic and geologic events may give rise to new life and new health. Give me a confidence that is open to the eons-long view.

For Reflection

- What catastrophic events in the world of nature have, in the end, brought about life and growth?
- What am I doing personally to become more attuned to the rhythms of nature rather than resistant to them?

25.

Deep Ecology

Mortals cannot abide in their pomp; they are like the animals that perish.
Ps 49: 12, 20

Deep ecologists, among others, point out the haughtiness of an anthropocentric view of the biosphere. Arne Naess, George Sessions, and Bill Devall have been among those who have advanced an "ecosophy," an Earth philosophy that de-centers the human and promotes what has been called "biocentric egalitarianism." Deep ecology does not presume that the human occupies a place of privilege and does not believe that humans have rights to override the "interests" of other beings to live and flourish merely in order to satisfy human whim, occupy human leisure, or gratify human obsession. Deep ecology argues that humans have no right to dominate, manipulate, displace, or drive to extinction. If deep ecology had its way, humans would all live more simply, less spaciously, more humbly, less exploitively.

While deep ecology can be critiqued for a disdain of human interests and an excess of enthusiasm for "otherkind," this school of thought does seem right in its observation that humans have often acted arrogantly and ignorantly in relation to the natural world—acting as though all its creatures and features were merely ornament and convenience, at the mercy of human pleasure.

This psalm, in reminding us of the transitoriness of human life and the mortality of the wise, along with "fool and dolt," points out that humans can never stake a lasting claim on land, waterways, or the skies. We are indeed "like the animals that perish," and, in the end, we own nothing. We are beneficiaries, and passing ones at that.

The Korahites, from whom this psalm comes, would have been a far cry from "biocentric egalitarianism," for the human is always, for them, the apple of God's eye. But their theocentric view of human relations and all creation calls us to a healthy humility and a tentativeness about what we name "ours." It is the nature of human beings to be outlasted by land and landscape. Ultimately there is nothing, this psalm reminds us, that we can keep.

God, you are our keeper. All that I have is temporarily mine to use in trust— for you and with you. Help me remember my place and my mortality, as you prevent me from clinging too tightly and staking fatuous claims.

For Reflection

- One of the salutary planks of the deep ecology "platform" fashioned by Naess and Sessions is a call for emphasis on "life quality" rather than "standard of living." How might I make some concrete efforts to downsize and simplify my lifestyle?
- One of the highly contested planks of the platform is a call for a drastic decrease in human population. Are there means, other than prevention of births, that can alter human patterns of consumption and exhaustion of resources?

26.

Vegetarianism?

"I will not accept a bull from your house or goats from your folds. For every wild animal of the forest is mine, the cattle on a thousand hills. I know all the birds of the air, and all that moves in the field is mine." **Ps 50:9–11**

Animal sacrifice is not the most common of practices in the United States, though there are always rumors about the clandestine practices of Satanism and voodoo. In many quarters people are embarrassed to wear fur, sharkskin, leather, or even the whimsical coonskin cap. Conferences, conventions, campuses, and retreat houses regularly offer vegetarian options for luncheon and banquet fare. Even McDonalds has its fruit 'n yogurt parfait as not only a dessert but a main course option. And Wendy's has a meal in a multi-topped potato.

We can argue endlessly about whether or not a vegetarian diet is the most healthful one. We can bicker about whether we should be semi-vegetarians; ovo-lacto-vegetarians getting our protein via yogurt, eggs, and cheese as well as soybeans and legumes; or vegans, renouncing any ingestion of animal products. We can also admit that vegetarianism is rather stylish. It's serious business and as spartan as the ancient lenten fast, but it is also a conversation starter and a fad. Those who are vegetarian for religious reasons are relatively few.

The psalmists and those who sang psalms on the climb to Jerusalem or in a time of lament would likely have regarded a strict vegetarian diet as a symptom of famine. They not only raised and tended livestock, but they also ate meat and offered prize, young fatlings as sacrifices to God. These sacrifices were signs of consecration, covenant, gratitude, and that loose grip which acknowledges that whatever we possess is transitory and, in the end, not ours. What God rails against, according to the testimony of psalm and Hebrew prophecy, is human arrogance, not human eating habits.

So, if we're to become vegetarians it ought to be for prophetic reasons. It ought to be a protest against capitalism's insistence that crops be raised for cattle to eat in order to produce gargantuan steaks, while indigenous people have their fields seized and are bereft of grain to fill a child's bowl. Our vegetarianism ought to be an act of solidarity with those who rarely see meat and have to get their iron from raisins. Our vegetarianism ought to be a choice against arrogance, a choice for simpler living. This includes eating lower on the food chain and repenting that much of our world cannot "super-size" anything.

Giver of food and drink, nourish me with the riches of your grains, nuts, vegetables, fruits, earthy oils. Make me one of the world's citizens who offer you praise and thanks for beans and rice.

For Reflection

- How do I eat? Do I savor gratefully? Do I season and spice? Do I know how to eat lean?
- If and when I fast, for what and for whom do I do it?

27.

The Clean Heart

Purge me with hyssop, and I shall be clean; wash me, and I shall be whiter than snow.
Ps 51:7

Hyssop is easily sliced to fashion a twiggy sprinkler. Branches, bushes, metal aspergilla serve the same purpose in rites that recall sin and baptism, contrition and forgiveness. The association of a few splashes of water with reviving and refreshment is obvious. We have often seen parched plants perk up at the merest touches of moisture. We ourselves have brushed dewy grass and shrubs in the early morning and have awakened. Stems and branches, we notice, have regained turgor after the slightest dewfall. We detect a shimmer and glisten in new day and morning light.

What we do not need is acid rain that eats at leaves, sullies our lakes, and threatens frogs with sterility. We do need clear dewdrops and trickles of rain that slake our taproots. When we come upon streams gorged with litter, muck, foam, and the overgrowth of algae caused by runoff from our chemically fertilized lawns, we groan. When we can see clear down through brook bubble and lake lap to slight undergrowth and stones, we feel clear, clean, relieved.

On the days around the ceremony that committed the ashes of John F. Kennedy, Jr., to the sea, his father's words were much quoted: "We are tied to the ocean. And when we go back to the sea, whether... it is to sail or to watch it, we are going back from whence we came."

As a species, we crawled up from ocean beds, unwrinkled our gills into smooth necks, and learned to breathe. As manchild and woman-child we floated and roiled first in womb water. Most of us took to our first baths and kiddie pools splashing. We learned to play in the liquid splay of garden hoses, fountains, and breaking waves.

We need our water safe, since it is among the earliest things we learn to trust.

And when we are soiled from the sweat and grit of the day, or when we are stained with our own sorry condition, we need our water free.

We need rainmakers and river watchers, Earth restorers and priests for the hyssop, the fronds, the freshening spray. We need those who love waterworks, since water is so much of what we are, and water is what recalls us to the swell and ebb of our clean beginnings.

God of birth and slaked thirst, teach me to better love your living water. Purify me in our usage. Hold me to a temperate enjoyment, a delight in the just enough that is so much. Give me play and reverent use.

For Reflection

- Robert F. Kennedy, Jr., has been a key player in Riverkeepers, Inc., an environmental group that keeps watch on the Hudson River and undertakes legal action against polluters. An underlying principle of the organization is obviously the environmental slogan, "Think globally, act locally." In my own locale, in my own home, what am I doing to conserve water and to keep water sources pure?
- What does the use of holy water, a sacramental, communicate to me?

28.

Wilderness and Eco-Action

Fear and trembling come upon me, and horror overwhelms me. And I say, "O that I had wings like a dove! I would fly away and be at rest; truly, I would flee far away; I would lodge in the wilderness; I would hurry to find shelter for myself from the raging wind and tempest." Ps 55:6–8

The 1994 film, *On Deadly Ground*, featuring Steven Seagal as eco-warrior and Michael Caine as greedy, driven eco-destroyer, depicts violent disregard for Alaskan waters and wildlife and Eskimos and the violent response that that evokes. The "hero" blows up people (mercenaries, the mendacious) and things (generators and oil rigs) wantonly, in defense of the land. What he most wants, though, is clear water, free ranges of ice and snow for polar bears and dog sleds and the eagle's line of sight.

The psalmist of yesteryear and the religious ecologist of today have more trust in law and the ultimate triumph of righteousness and good than Seagal's character, "Forest," did. He acted as law unto himself and, yes, "won" the land back from waste and illness and oil spills, but he did it with force, foolhardiness, explosives, and bloodshed.

The spirit of the psalm, with its sense that "the bloodthirsty and treacherous shall not live out half their days" (v 23), is more the spirit of those of us who belong to moderate environmental groups—the

Nature Conservancy, the Sierra Club, etc. We use influence, media coverage, purchases, and legal action to bring down despoilers. This way seems fairer, more effective in the long run, more godly. We appeal to reason and, even if eco-threats are imminent, to a certain amount of patient waiting for the forces of destruction to begin, as they inevitably do, to undo themselves. Those of us whose ecological stance is religious wait also for God to act in nature, in God's own time, and through our nonviolence.

We do, however, acknowledge enmity. Buttery speech does not belong only to the ancient opponents of David (v 21). It is the spin and the advertising style of auto companies, installers of pipelines, land "developers," oil refinery owners, and spokespersons for nuclear power plants. We cannot trust their word, or their take on events and effects.

So we turn to blessed wilderness for refreshment, restoration, vistas where we can see clearly, airy landscapes in which we can breathe freely and hear the sounds of night and dawning. We fly to these unsullied places where we can regain calm and retrain our resolve.

In such places there are always trees, living water sources, nesting places, and the scatterings of spirit and folk wisdom, Hebrew, Inuit, or our own.

God of life, lead me to know when fight is called for and when flight is well-timed. Help me face forces of destruction with steady resistance and stand for preservation and ecojustice with confidence and trust. Give me simple spots wherein to center, and wildernesses wherein to renew.

For Reflection

- What and where are the power centers in nature that strengthen me for good, for endurance, for needed confrontation?
- What have I done to help preserve wilderness, wildlife, and natural habitats?

29.

Borne Away

Sooner than your pots can feel the heat of thorns, whether green or ablaze, may he sweep them away! **Ps 58:9**

The besieged singer of Psalm 58 makes his wish for enemies: that they blow away like sliced off thorn branches, or like thistles cut from their green stalk, their full purple-headed strength washed down to a pale off-white, their petals sapped of turgor and substance.

The wish, however, has its irony, a spiteful side. For thorn bushes prickle and choke, and thistles spread as virulently as purple loosestrife, the tall wildflower that has overtaken Michigan's roadsides and wetlands. New thistles can beset fields and outgrow cornflowers, clover, daisies, and brown-eyed susans. Their insubstantial fringes scatter in wind and multiply and multiply. The effect is not the best for local ecosystems. Similarly, the renumbering and exponential growth of enemies is nothing a human can want to pray for. It might be understandable, though, if one prays for the sterility of enemies, for some genetic mutation that leaves them seedless.

We can blow all sorts of things far and away: drooping petals, wavering spider webs, unpleasant memories, the unease of realities we wish were not. We can wish away signs of conflict, cultural degradation, deleterious climate change. We can also be our own enemies.

We dare to hope that we aren't blithely caught in the unexpected whirlwind, especially not one we've bidden. Or especially not one we have blown off as insignificant.

Much of your creation, Lord, regenerates and spreads, disappears and fades, and then resurges elsewhere. Some of your creation sticks and tears away. So too do my deeds, for good or ill. Let me take caution, Lord, from the lessons of your thorns and thistles.

For Reflection

- Some earthwatchers suggest that the wild, destructive weathers of the 1990s and early 2000s—the relentless summer heat, East coast droughts, West coast mudslides, battering tornadoes and hurricanes, blizzards—are the result of human-induced global warming. If indeed these are signs that we humans have transgressed against the planet's stability, what am I called to do in response? Is there any undoing that I can effect for the sake of well-being? Are there unhealthy attitudes, or is there any enmity, that I bear toward the innocents of the created world?

30.

~~~~~~

Rock Formations

For God alone my soul waits in silence; from him comes my salvation. He alone is my rock and my salvation, my fortress. I shall never be shaken. **Ps 62:1–2**

A triad of rocks sits just south of the herb garden at Seven Ponds Nature Center in Dryden, Michigan. The large rock, striated granite laced with pink and dull ochre, could easily hold a few sitters. The sitters would have to be agile, though, capable of kneeing over and straddling edges and hump. The smaller rocks are darker, one of them good for the adult sitter who can face the late day sun; the other, the mossy one, a good size for the sitting child, squat enough for short legs to touch the ground.

St. Thomas Aquinas, seven centuries ago, professed his faith that all creatures "bear the trace of the Trinity" (ST I.45.7). We might conjecture that certain arrangements of creatures can too. Thus, the observer can find something Trinitarian in this triangle of rocks. The large, angled, planed, striped, tougher-to-negotiate but sure and steady-as-centuries rock can be designated the Maker of the Universe rock. The smallest one, worn, muddied, mossy, planted deep in Earth life and encircled with swallowing grasses and weeds, is the Christ rock, ever accessible and welcoming to the child. The adult size rock has room for two, if one is a small person, and the sitter can choose to face north, south, east, or west. In the sun, the rock warms well but is not too hot to touch. The dragonfly idles by, and the ant traverses one of its small crevices. The breeze catches grass blade and the sitter's blouse and hair. It is a good rock for *zazen*, philosophic thought, artistic vision, poetic play, or Christian prayer—a Spirit rock.

More than anything, these rocks promise to persist—longer than the Center, longer than the strollers and sitters, longer than the Audubon Society, the company of friends, the small family, longer even than the American nation. The rocks are and long have been. They are inscrutable yet definite as solidity and weight. They are subtly multicolored yet simply gray.

The rocks are, in other words, as complex as divinity and as shrouded in mystery, since we can only guess their stories. Yet they are altogether prominent, accessible, as ordinary as the impulse to touch and sit.

God of the convenient and everlasting rocks, let me seize your invitations to be still, to sit a while, to remember that I too am passing, while much that you have made is eons long. Let me recall that I am a worldling, connected and kin to the matter that makes rock, yet also drawn and spirited off by mementoes of you.

For Reflection

- What natural formations or configurations of rock, forests, sands, or lake have put me in touch with God?
- To what centers or preserves might I go in order to be free to catch the traces of the Trinity?

31.

Drought Scenes

O God,... my soul thirsts for you; my flesh faints for you, as in a dry and weary land where there is no water. **Ps 63:1**

When a medical test requires that we refrain from food and water from midnight on, we find the hours almost unbearable. When we have a dehydrating gastro-intestinal infection, our electrolytes go off kilter, and we sink into weakness and confusion. And when we are irrevocably dying, when we no longer can sustain intravenous or a deep draught of anything, small swabs to suck are our final comfort. Inevitably, we fever and can taste our own salt.

Drought is unendurable unless some water hole is found, unless some source of water is trucked and helicoptered in. We shrivel. We become like ash. Our flesh becomes November leaf, brittle and crumbling.

We can thirst for many things—for knowledge, for love, for achievement, for glory, for God. But there can be nothing more rapidly debilitating than unslaked physical thirst.

When environmentalists warn that we risk desertification by our clear-cutting, road building, dam erecting, lawn watering, Vegas-settling, Phoenix-sprawling, we need to take heed. A drink may, a decade or less away, be a very precious commodity.

You tell me, God, that you give ease and that you fill the hunger and thirst of those who long for you. Help me long for you in such a way that I save clean water for my neighbors, friends, and the numberless unknowns who share my watershed, and those who will.

For Reflection

- Worldwatch's annual State of the World Report, in its 2003 edition, cited the way in which the desertification of China has caused dust storms in South Korea. It also notes a 2001 United Nations report that reservoirs worldwide can store less and less water as human construction causes more and more erosion and sedimentation. The same 2003 edition also urges, in a chapter by Gary Gardner, that the world's religions ought to be using their spiritual force to help their members engage environmental issues more forcefully. (See "Engaging Religion in the Quest for a Sustainable World.") When I hear alarming news about the global effects of human behavior, what is my response? How do my religious beliefs affect this response?

32.

Diligent Abundance

You visit the earth and water it,...softening it with showers, and blessing its growth.... The pastures of the wilderness overflow, the hills gird themselves with joy, the meadows clothe themselves with flocks, the valleys deck themselves with grain, they shout and sing together for joy. Ps 65:9, 10, 12–13

There are places lush with life that have been made so by design. The Frederick Meijer Gardens outside Grand Rapids, Michigan, host multitudes of birds—all kinds of parakeets and finches, along with Chinese quail and the pintailed whydah, whose tail flushes to three times its body length in breeding season. It's the whydah form of exultation. Cherry trees, black cherries, sugar maples, red maples, oaks, and long grasses edge the walks and woods. Indoors, bamboo grows.

At the Orchard Lake Nature Sanctuary, a quick right off Pontiac Trail, one meets, in a few square miles, small wonders: pines dropping cones from lofty heights, a prairie of wildflowers, toadstools jutting out like saucers and plates from tree trunks, goldenrod, thistles, brown-eyed ewer, wild grape vine, wild raspberries, barberry, myrtle, woodland creeper, lily of the valley, witch hazel; and chipmunks; and one slim snake in a sortie onto the Yellow Trail (or the Red, or the Blue).

"There are fungus among us," quips a walker. In the heavy shade, an all-time shade, it is a surprise that there are so many green and flowering things. The forest floor holds the damp of rain and the humid hints of the nearby lake. The tell-tale sign: mildew on picnic benches and sign-boards. The human concessions barely mar the scene, though. These gardens and sanctuaries are holy places, temples reaching hosanna high.

The song that is Psalm 65 unashamedly personifies. It has hills and meadows and valleys dressing up for a party, a festival, then breaking into shout and song. Nature stamps and claps hands.

The heart of praise is life bursting out all about, the psalm reveals. Sometimes structure and human help are required to keep a woodland sanctuary. Sometimes human voices must declare, "This far and no farther," for the sake of a holy of holies. Barberry. Myrtle. Woodland creeper. A snake sidling into song. A whydah fanning its tail to court.

Praise to you, God of the raspberry bush and black cherry. Joy to you, land living in space sacred and free.

For Reflection

- What is the nature preserve, public garden, or sanctuary closest to me? Do I support it? Visit it? Go sometimes to hear its hymns?

33.

Invitatory

May God be gracious to us and bless us and make his face to shine upon us. Ps 67:1

Short, straightforward, succinct: that's an adequate description of this psalm. Ask God for blessing and God-shine. Say hooray because we already know God's walk, God's way, just judgment, guidance, and we want to show it off again. So, thank you, God, for all of it, over and over, and also this time.

New Haven Lighthouse stands tall, solid, whitewashed stone with a black-framed top, set on a high shoreline dune amid several miles of stone jetties, buoys, and channel markers. The winds off the river and Long Island Sound groan and batter around it. On a sunny April afternoon, the wide inlet glistens, sequined. The lighthouse served past navigators well. Now it makes a park and tourist attraction. Swing sets range the Sound side, set among cement sculptures of dolphins and great tortoises. There are picnic pavilions east, and ball fields. Just off to the right of the lighthouse is a rock-braced telescopic stand, offering views for coins. The sand is flecked with gravel, gull leavings, shells. It inevitably gets combed.

But the park is all about the lighthouse. It has beckoned newcomers, guided pilots to safe haven, and fixed bittersweet memories for families.

One memorial to Harvey Barque offers a slogan in French: Let the good times roll. Another plaque remembers Steven M. Smith, a serviceman, dead at twenty-nine, shown as a youth in uniform and as a rollicking man in a cowboy hat.

Lighthouse Park is a place for light: love light, child light, sunset, God light. One can walk here with someone slowly, hand in hand. Or one can offer a psalm in solitude, wondering how we got from God's command, "Let there be light," to Zechariah's messianic canticle, marking the onset of Christ light, to a nation of commerce, invention, prosperity, warfare, and night life. U.S. 1, I–95, I–91 parallel and curve off nearby, always under light.

On a park bench, along the shore of a quieted New Haven Light, we may ask, though, for purer light. And the simpler havens that were and can be.

Let your face, yes, let it shine on us. Amid every other light. Day and night.

For Reflection

- The lights of lighthouses may require surprisingly low wattage. It's the mirrors and prisms that magnify, magnify. What does that say to me about life lights? What about the light that shines from me?
- God's "face," in ancient scripture, is blinding, the sight of it even deadly. What light awes me? What light endangers me? Us?
- What kind of light do I find most emblematic of God?

34.

Inundation

Save me, O God, for the waters have come up to my neck. I sink in the deep mire, where there is no foothold; I have come into deep waters, and the flood sweeps over me. **Ps 69:1**

There are everglades, marshlands, swamps, quicksand, places where we can leave no tracks. There are dank, dark spots where we can be swallowed alive. At Silver Sands Beach, outside Milford, Connecticut, stern warnings are posted. At low tide it's possible to walk all the way to a small, vine-knotted island. At high tide, though, watch! The entire sandbar floods over. A cleaving undertow develops. Even the gulls get knocked about as their gravelly perches disappear.

Prophets among us warn that we can drown in our own success. We can be sucked up to our heads in our luxuries and entitlements. Note our tastefully furnished and fully equipped time shares, travel lodges, and motels with daily change of bed linens and oversize towels, their cable connections for TV and Internet, the personal percolators and hair dryers. Note our acres of storage garages. Observe how we rate comfort and prosperity in terms of the square footage of our residences and offices and their closet size. The amenities of first class travel barely move us, nor does the complimentary paper delivered daily to a hotel door. Prayer breakfasts and business lunches are so sumptuous that they might overwhelm the glutton. We throw the untouched food away.

There's so little we can spare for the poor. Welfare is inefficient. It creates dependencies. We cluck over the shame of the working poor as we close the polling curtains behind us and vote to unseam their safety net laws. Elder care facilities risk bankruptcy as we slice away at Medicaid reimbursements and manage away the once good payback of Medicare Part A.

Our shoulders shrug, and our limbs set, motionless. We're stuck in a muck that looks like uneaten dinners, cast off clothes, creased vacation brochures, and dented toys. Save us, O God, we ask.

Save me, God, from slime of my own making. Give me zeal, really, for the clear land of your truth.

For Reflection

- One thing about these psalms of asking: the answer is in the ask. Before we've pursed our lips for the last word, the need is met, the deed done. What does our consumer culture need most of God these days? Dare I ask?

- This psalm can be read as the serious outcry of one falsely accused, as a plea of the righteous for justification and truth. Or it can be read ironically, as the prayer of the self-satisfied, the petition of the clueless who don't even notice that they've stolen from the poor and wrought damages that anger the deprived. How does the psalm go if I read it that way?

35.

Future Generations

So even to old age and gray hairs,... do not forsake me, until I proclaim your might to all the generations to come. **Ps 71:18**

A topic of contention among environmental ethicists has been the question of whether future generations can be said to have "rights." Are we duty bound to leave healthy habitats and clean water and air to beings yet to come? Do we owe the "integrity, beauty, and stability" of our local bioregion (see Aldo Leopold's "Land Ethic") to future humans who might (or might not) choose to live there? Do we owe anything to prospective groundhogs, deer, raccoons, finches, robins, apple trees, forsythia, marsh grass, or to upcoming droplets in river or creek?

Common sense suggests, ethical debates aside, that the human yearning for a future ought to lead us to bequeath a good Earth to those who come after us. Religious faith suggests that, if we hope to pass on faith in a benevolent Creator, we must assure that future generations can see why creation, in its multiplicity and diversity, has been deemed "good."

The question of future generations is about their health and well being, then. We look to hand on the good life and harmonious surroundings for the sake of others. It's a sort of inherent altruism. It's also our psychological need to be generative, to leave that which is worthwhile after us. But it's also reverence. We recall that Earth and all dwelling therein are not our own. We cannot rightly deplete or exhaust Earth, or our small neighborhoods of it, without being godless.

Anne Matthews, in the concluding chapter of *Wild Nights: Nature Returns to the City*, presents several scenarios of what New York City might be like in 2050. The worst-case scenario sees it toxic and rotting, battered by hurricanes and blizzards brought on by global warming, and habitable by few species. The best-case scenario sees it consistently warmer, flooded at the lower end of Manhattan, bereft of familiar shorelines, and more hospitable to the peregrine falcons, horseshoe crabs, and coyotes that are already reclaiming the city. What prompts the dismal picture? Much of Manhattan is built on landfill; its population is denser than a small island can bear; it has had problems with water purification, air quality, sewage treatment, and waste disposal for decades—actually, well over a century. And the Earth seems irreversibly to be warming.

Some of what has been done can't be undone. But a God who calls us to "choose life" and to proclaim the good of creation equips us to plan ahead, modify, redress. We can live more lightly.

We may not be able to solve the "rights" question to the satisfaction of philosophical ethicists. But we can be very sure that it is possible for wrongs to be done to generations who don't yet exist.

Help me, God, think not even so far as to the seventh generation. Help me think of the second, third, and fourth to come when I buy, build, use.

For Reflection

- What do I hope my current neighborhood, town or city, and bioregion might be like in 2050? What do I fear it might become?
- What can I do to help assure that it will be livable and healthful for generations to come?

36.

Flourishing

May there be an abundance of grain in the land; may it wave on the tops of the mountains; may its fruit be like Lebanon; and may people blossom in the cities like the grass of the field. Ps 72:16

Psalm 72 is an extended prayer for the reign of a splendid leader and for the flourishing of a messianic realm. It describes the Hebrew notion of "shalom": general and generous well being, abundant crops, beautiful land, healthy families, harmonious interactions, and relations that yield lasting peace.

Humanity has hoped for this for thousands, for hundreds of thousands of years, it seems. We have not yet learned how to achieve it for any sustained period even in biblical lands. We fight for oil wells and against toxic weaponry in the land of the Tigris and Euphrates, the cradle of creation, according to Genesis. We hear daily of rock throwing, gun butt pummeling, car bombings, bus bombings between and among Palestinians and Israelis. Where is there milk and honey in the Promised Land? Christians pilot Apache helicopters and launch "bunker-busting" missiles as though there had never been a birth of the Prince of Peace. Whence shalom, and where might it come from?

Future wars, some say, will be fought over water. Others say they will be fought over land as millions of refugees flee flooded shorelines, as rivers and oceans rise and rise and rise.

The prophet Micah says of the Messiah that "he shall be peace" (Mi 5:4). We say the Messiah has come. The Messiah is. This Messiah blesses the peacemakers.

We hold the Messiah's world in our hands. It behooves us to find creative ways, hard-won ways, patient yet painstaking ways, to resolve conflicts and to make shalom.

Make me, God, a peacemaker in every way. For you. For me. For us. For a whole world of being.

For Reflection

- The best way to give children a sense of hope for the future and a conviction that peace is possible is to talk about and share with them what we're doing to make the world a better place. What, then, is my peace project? What have I done today on behalf of shalom?

37.

Deliverance

Do not deliver the soul of your dove to the wild animals; do not forget the life of your poor forever. **Ps 74:19**

The Mercy Center in Madison, Connecticut, opens onto Long Island Sound, to an expanse of rising and falling sea, vistas of distant lighthouses and nearby ducks and loons gliding from rock mass to rock mass, gulls swerving and swooping. At this serene retreat center one can spend days in silence, craft one's prayer in clay or haiku or finger paint or flute song, pace a labyrinth, or tell twenty decades of the rosary. There are cushions inviting a long sit by the indoor tabernacle, and benches set amid pines outside inviting *zazen*.

It's hard to recall at such a place that we are not so far upstream (or up I-95) from Wall Street, from the ruins of the World Trade Center, from the headquarters of NBC, ABC, CBS, and the spin of reports on which sites the U.S. has most recently invaded or bombed.

Aggression persists. It is native to our species. Vows of nonviolence—and their intricate practicum—don't come easily. Some of us, frankly, can't eschew all violence, even if we admire Mahatma Gandhi, Thomas Merton, Dorothy Day, and the El Salvador martyrs with all our souls.

Children are taught to take "time out" before turning to slapping and fisticuffs. We need to enforce time out for adults, for ourselves, before we hit; before we demoralize; before we tear up our countryside or anyone else's. Before we cheer on the bombs-away mentality. Before we leave cities and countries a desert waste. Before we conclude that negotiation, compromise, mediation are passé.

We need places where lapping tides, clouds, seabirds, and sunrises can still our souls; and where peace prayers can be offered day after day, night after night, by rosary bead, by labyrinth walk, by sanctuary lamp, by verse or line, by candlelight.

Let me find, make, cherish, make offerings to your centers of peace. Deliver me, my God.

For Reflection

- When the pressure is on, when I'm exasperated or enraged or both, what gives me pause before I explode?
- What settings restore perspective and calm for me?
- Not everything in nature is nonviolent. There is aggression, competition, conflict among many life forms. What lessons can I learn about humanity from observing nature's violence and nonviolence?

38.

Lightning Strike

The crash of your thunder was in the whirlwind; your lightnings lit up the world; the earth trembled and shook. **Ps 77:18**

In *A Match to the Heart,* Gretel Ehrlich offers a gripping autobiographical account of being struck by lightning and then struggling for months to regain a measure of life and health. It takes time to walk, she learned. It takes time to regain confidence in sudden sounds. It takes time to keep from being utterly panic-stricken by the first faint boom of distant thunder.

There's a strange beauty in lightning, the zig and zag of light, the quick flash in blue-black night, the syncopation of thunder roll and strike. The ancient Slovaks prayed to Zun and Perun, the gods of lightning and thunder. They prayed to appease them, to spare thatched huts and stores of corn husks and vagrant children unwarily flitting amid raindrops near trees.

Ehrlich barely knew that she was hit. She didn't grasp that her heart was nearly stopped by electric shock. She began to piece together the story only through a long recovery. What she learned was more than the power of lightning.

She learned the suddenness and arbitrariness of life. She learned from inside out the insight of Quohelethl: "Vanity of vanities…" is the sum of our control, our well-laid plans. She learned the reason why Buddhism teaches the indeterminacy of reality and illusion. Why it emphasizes the importance of being with what is.

All of the great religions, all mysticism, somehow come down to a simple acceptance of life on its own terms. Non-graspingness. Non-management. It's a counter-intuitive and counter-cultural lesson.

Sometimes it takes life's flicker. Sometimes it takes a moment when we aren't certain whether the flame will restart or pass, hissing, out.

I remember, God, an accident or two. I recall how I unwittingly let go. Help me, God, seize the power of powerlessness and so grow.

For Reflection

- Have I met, face to face, a near-death experience or spent time with someone who has? If so, how does such an experience change a person?
- The fact of our mortality causes grief, fear, dismay. How do I regard death? Am I able to contemplate my own?
- Lightning is among many natural wonders that bear a frightful beauty. What other dangerous things do I find carrying an eerie loveliness? Can I love a God who makes some beauty a threat and terror to me?

39.

Interventions

In the daytime he led them with a cloud, and all night long with a fiery light. He split rocks open in the wilderness, and gave them drink abundantly as from the deep. He made streams come out of the rock, and caused waters to flow down like rivers.
Ps 78:14–16

A sanctuary haloed in light. Sprays of red, yellow, white mums, candles in red and vanilla glass. A circle of bread mounted in a stand with golden arms. An occasional draught of cool from the edges of stained glass windows. It's a late autumn afternoon, and the chapel is a site for eucharistic devotions. Shoulders and heads rise above the backs of pews, and we all sit gazing.

God piques and focuses our senses and calls us to things here and now. We make mosaics, carve altars from marble, fashion furnishings of oak, make tiles, shape glass, and color our inner sanctums in perfect circles and diamonds and rectangles. Bird shapes and vine forms remind us that we live in a sacramental universe.

All that we are and all that is partake of God, we say. God asserts Godself, summons our attention, and offers a few moments of taste and comfort by way of simple things. We pick some flowers, form flat circles of wheat, ferment grapes, and sing.

Whether it is our small votive lights or cloud by day and fire by night, creatures whisper to us that God is close by.

We believe, that is, if we trust in a God of life. A swing of incense says, oh, yes, there are heavens above, far galaxies, a spirit world, and mysteries. But whatever is there—and honored here—is also now. And with. And quiet as holy hours.

Give me, God, the simple, whispered OH that can stir my everyday soul.

For Reflection

- How have my senses been blessed today? And when divinely?
- A benediction, a blessing, often seems an end to ceremony. In what sense is it simply part of a series?
- Do I believe that we live in a sacramental universe? (It's an expression the American Catholic bishops have used.)

40.

After Annihilation

Do not remember against us the iniquities of our ancestors; let your compassion come speedily to meet us, for we are brought very low. **Ps 79:8**

The Diary of Anne Frank, Schindler's List, The Pianist. These films—and there are certainly more to come—remind us of Hitler's holocaust. The blitz, the death camps, the seduction of Germany are horrors we can't forget. So, too, are Pearl Harbor, the unleashing of atomic bombs on Hiroshima and Nagasaki. Amid it all, Mussolini and the siege of Leningrad are almost lost. Stalin. The massacres at Katyn.

We remember and revere those whom Tom Brokaw has called "the greatest generation," the service men and women who are now eighty and ninety years old, and the ones who have passed on and whose flags are replaced or renewed each Memorial Day. Those who live we take care of. We help them downsize and move closer to family so they can get some ready help. We double, triple, quadruple our retirement communities to provide a continuum of care—independent living in cottages and apartments, assisted living in cozy suites, Alzheimer's care in "Wondergard" protected annexes and white-fenced yards, skilled nursing care in expansive, bright, spanking new facilities. We put landscaped patios and window boxes in view of windows built low enough that they afford a wheelchair view. We bring patios indoors, creating patio simulators in parlor space. Huge aquariums let our seniors watch the sallyings forth of nibbling fish. Friendly dogs come in on their assigned days for petting. Amazing aviaries, rich in songbirds and color, appear in the complexes' lobbies.

A generation that has seen world war, concentration camp, radiation sickness, and five to six decades more of sputtering genocide and global conflict deserves innocent pleasures, a restoration of childlike wonder in flowers, fish, dogs, birds, ficus trees.

And what of us? Homicide and biocide have not ceased. We call occasional moratoriums and then find new wars to wage, new damages to be done. Will loving nature heal us? Will our brief visits to marinas, zoos, seaside resorts, winter lakes, and nature centers equip us with enough enthusiasm for life to save it? Will movies admonish us sternly enough to learn from our errors and to prevent their repetition?

We ask for God's compassion. We construct peaceful sites for our elders' last days, places where they can simplify and forget what battered and beset their youth. What, though, do we do to spare God's people and Earth's creatures from our iniquities?

War no more, God. Make me a celebrant of life. Please.

For Reflection

- What mistakes of the Greatest Generation do I regret? What heroism do I admire?
- If I were to enumerate the sins of the elders that my generation has repeated, how would I number them?
- What moves me to compassion? Where do I need to be more moved?

41.

David, Sun and Moon

I will not lie to David. His line shall continue forever, and his throne endure before me like the sun. It shall be established forever like the moon, an enduring witness in the skies.
Ps 89:35–37

We think of David as the ruddy, unsuspecting sheepherder snatched away from his family by the prophet Samuel. We think of him as the giant-slayer and then the harpist whose soft song could not assuage a crazed king. We think of him as psalmist and dancer before the Ark of the Covenant. We remember him, too, as a passionate man, in love with life, his people, his people's God, his several wives and the lustrous wife of Uriah. We know him as a man who repents his own adultery and murder. And we know him as a man who laments the death of his soul friend, Jonathan, and of his rebellious son, Absalom, Absalom.

David is our alter ego. His are our loves, our longings, our creative energies, our devotions, our achievements, our disappointments, our resourcefulness, our griefs, our sins multiplied by at least ten, maybe by 3,000.

David danced by day and bedded by night. David slew by day and prayed by night. Even when he slipped into shadow, though, he never seemed completely to lose the light. There was always a path to find, a green pasture in which to rest. A sturdy tree to lean on, a rock on which to gain a foothold, and the heavens to gaze upon.

David found all around him the inescapability of God. He found God's "enduring witness in the skies."

From him came Mary, "a woman clothed with the sun, with the moon under her feet, and on her head a crown of twelve stars" (Rev 12:1). From him came her son, the Sun-God, the morning star, the Easter dawn. David's son. The Son whose light we are called to be, too.

God of light, break upon me. God of light, lead my way. God of sun and moon, bathe me in your inescapability and make of me, too, your enduring witness in the skies.

For Reflection

- When have daybreak or moonrise been part of my religious experience?
- What do I find most moving in the Easter Vigil liturgy?
- What in my life is David's? What isn't?

42.

❧❧❧

Sabbath and the Realm of Time

For a thousand years in your sight are like yesterday when it is past, or like a watch in the night. **Ps 90:4**

Sabbaths begin in gardens, like Eden, or the garden near the empty tomb donated by Joseph of Arimathea. Mary Magdalene encounters the risen Christ in the early morning and mistakes him for a gardener.

"Let me look upon a garden. I shall catch a glimpse of God." That message is inscribed at the entry to Sunny Meadow Garden Gallery in Dryden, Michigan. It's a place where one can stroll through long outdoor rows of shade plants, herbs, perennials, or gaze upon the potted flowers, cacti, succulents, bonsai exhibited inside. Rev. Donna Schaper recommends summer gardens and winter gardens in her book *Sabbath Sense: A Spiritual Antidote for the Overworked*.

With the rabbi Jesus, Schaper reminds us that the Sabbath was made for us. It was meant to disengage us from our clockwork rituals, to throw us off our timeclock rhythms, to slow us, rest us, and open us to God.

Gardens, art museums, symphonies, liturgical celebrations are all meant to unbalance us a bit. Sabbaticals are intended to give us the long view, to rest us and then reset us on the path of purposiveness, lending new productivity to our life-projects.

Our faith-span, after all, is measured in millennia, not the minutes of our eight or twelve or fourteen-hour workdays. In our 24-7 culture, it is increasingly difficult to reappropriate Sabbath, that time of family, worship, play. We're able to log on, check in, access and be accessed, eat out, pick up the building materials for a project at Home Depot, and wander the shopping mall on weekend and weekday alike.

What we need, say Schaper and John Paul II (in *Dies Domini*) is to take back our watches of the night, those times when we can't quite tell what time it is (unless we illuminate our watch and clock faces), when deep blue-black shadows lull us to sleep, when we can hear the crash of tide but not see the horizon line, when senses slow as we study the expanse and distance of starry sky.

We need, too, to reclaim one day a week, so that we might pad through a garden conversing with a friend. So that we might be God's children and never hear the tick-tock in the crocodile innards. So that we can see that someone we know looks like someone else by morning light when we're taking time.

Out of time and beyond our borders, call me, God, to your quiet, your restoration, and to perspective on my stress.

For Reflection

- What helps me regain perspective on the workaday world and relax my frazzled nerves?
- What hobbies provide my personal therapy?
- How does worship orient me to a different sense of time?

43.

Uprightness

The righteous flourish like the palm tree and grow like a cedar in Lebanon.... In old age they still produce fruit; they are always green and full of sap, showing that the Lord is upright. Ps 92:12, 14–15

Thomas Merton, the Trappist monk and prolific writer who was guru to contemplatives, conventuals, and social activists of the 1950s and 1960s, is remembered for his ongoing dialogue with the world. From monastery and hermitage, he kept up steady conversation about the importance of silence, woodlands, liturgical prayer, and the rightness of racial justice and the disarmament movements. He plumbed Scripture, Catholic tradition, the wisdom of Gandhi, and Zen to learn what was instructive, good, and peaceable to all. He had wed himself to God on behalf of the world's people.

It may be somewhat surprising, then, to find Merton declaring, "The silence of the forest is my bride and the sweet dark warmth of the whole world is my love" (*Dancing in the Water of Life*, quoted by Kathleen Deignan, ed., in *When the Trees Say Nothing*). Merton found that silence, poverty, chastity, obedience, *conversio morum* led him in and out simultaneously: in to his own depths, in to wordlessness and truth, in to the heart of God, then out to comprehend history, to attend to everything present, to warn and hope of things to come. Merton found a largeness of Christ, a universality of the risen one, in the most particular of persons, places, things.

We can know the same, even if in fragments. A visit to an adoration chapel or a fifteen-minute candle-lit, muted prayer for peace somehow invites the whole world in. A browse through Zen poems and their notes reveals to us that the Japanese word for pine is *matsu* and that the word also means "I will wait for you." Suddenly we understand why we have been drawn to one sturdy pine, why we have sketched it and colored it. God simply had something to say in pine, and conspired for us to uncover the clue.

We're steadied by word and world. Trees endure longer than we do. They signify enlightenment and salvation history. They remind us in some sense to be tree: to stand firm, to give a little, to shelter, to shed, to bud, to bear. To wait for someone.

Lord, let me age in wisdom and grace. Let me grow rings of love, widening out and out.

For Reflection

- Where do trees figure in my personal faith history?
- Where are my favorite tree places?
- Where am I growing? In what way, regardless of my age, am I "green and full of sap"?

44.

Becoming Praise

Let the heavens be glad, and let the earth rejoice; let the sea roar, and all that fills it; let the field exult, and everything in it. Then shall all the trees of the forest sing for joy before the Lord; for he is coming. **Ps 96:11–13**

The Oriental Garden in the northeast corner of the Cranbrook Gardens in Bloomfield Hills, Michigan, surrounds a wide-mouthed pool which surely and serenely gulps water that bubbles and streams over a short waterfall. A wooden gate, with two exalted, gently bent limbs making its archway and two tree trunks supporting the concave arch, frames the entry steps to the graveled path. Green plants with leaves as large as elephant ears grow there amid delicate reeds, magenta and sun-yellow flowers, drowsy, leaning, soft-leaved pines, and orange tinged maple, and something reminiscent of bonsai. Every twenty minutes or so a single fish leaps from the pool and drips back into a circular splash point. Across blue sky, where puffs of cumulus flow east, a wide winged bird heads wood-ward.

Natural fields and forests so explode with life that they are rendered celebrant whether we eye them or not. Cultivated gardens are their own reason for being, yet also ours. We can fix on the tufted shrub that rises from rock, the branch-long crawl of gingko leaves, the long grasses that edge an artesian well where bamboo pipe drips into a large stone bowl. We can watch fish and fowl one by one and let the beauty of movement, breath, wind waft, rustling branches fall into our open souls. In the garden we deliberately, fixedly have made a spot for stillness and for praise.

Praise and thanks are what we are so much made for and what we so often bypass and neglect. Praise is also what the living do. Being still, flourishing in our garden spots, drinking in what is, pleasuring ourselves in sunlight and air are our reception of gift and our gift back. There is a gladness of xylem, phloem, bird whistle, fish bone. We listen, and they sing.

Maker of all life forms, inspirer of our urge for sacred spots and ambience, call us to attention. Give us the impulse to listen and the art to make moments among your soft, fringed, and floating things. Raise our silence into praise that joins them.

For Reflection

- Throughout the psalms, there appear *tehillah*, praise songs. Not only human beings but also the great variety of living creatures are said to praise God. The implication is that all things praise God by their very being. How might I praise God wordlessly? What acts of mine might introduce dissonance into the songs of praise around me?

45.

❧❧❧

The Tumble-Down

His lightnings light up the world; the earth sees and trembles. The mountains melt like wax before the Lord, before the Lord of all the earth. **Ps 97:4–5**

Every now and then some lava flows. Every now and then some lightning crackles and enflames the better part of a state. Mount St. Helen's. Pinatuba. Etna. Colorado wildfire. The paradox of a rainforest burning in Indonesia.

We don't choose to worship a god of destruction, a Vishnu, a god of breakdown.

We do choose, however, to worship a God who creates, makes new, transforms. And we find that, in God's design, the natural world does not remain static. It moves, it rearranges itself, it burns some forests off, it spills from hot innards and blows ash about. The results may not be attractive. They may, in fact, wreak misery and death on humans and others.

God's power is not in the chaos, the prophets say. The power is in the aftermath. God's Earth has lifetimes to make something new of its dust and debris. We, meanwhile, lament.

The wonder is that we can sometimes regard natural disasters as natural wonders. The wonder is that we can sometimes take a long view.

God, rescue me before I burn. Keep me in faith and out of harm's way.

For Reflection

- Consider a time when some destructive natural event transformed a place or a people positively.
- In the scale of disasters, what do you find most devastating—artificial, human-caused disasters or natural ones? Why? What disasters can we prevent? Are there some we ought to let happen as they will?
- Where is God when fire, flood, hurricane, tornado, earthquake, and volcanic eruption befall us?

46.

Loneliness Surrounded

I am like an owl of the wilderness, like a little owl of the waste places. I lie awake: I am like a lonely bird on the housetop. **Ps 102:6–7**

It may be a plaintive, elongated hoot at night, a coo and another coo and another coo uttered from dense branches amid a dark grove. Moon may strike the forested night and cast a long shadow. No one knows, though, quite where the owl perches or what its longings are. Its round, though, we know, the round of waking, seed and insect and rodent seeking, mating, nesting, bearing, feeding, sleeping, sinking into a fur of feathers, lidding large owl eyes, waking again, beginning again the seeking, mating, nesting, bearing, and feeding, slipping amid sometime glint of sun and sometime glint of eyes.

Our own loneliness draws us to understand this, sometimes nearly to despair of it. We do our small living. We make our small noise. We repeat ourselves and our small needs.

There is a world out there—of ash to eat and sometimes bread, of grass to water and sometimes burn, of shadows to dodge and sometimes embrace, of wine to sip and sometimes tears.

Much passes: days, night, loves, familiar places, lives. Grace, they say, stays. Life force. Eternal verities. The swing of seasons. Change. We can be surrounded by aliveness yet unknowing. The owl does not know that we hear. We do not know who or what is affected by our sighs or mutterings in the night. We do not see the clay-colored toad emerge and squat on the moonlit road. We do not note when the night primroses begin to spin shut. The seed does not know whether it will sprout or feed. The world of one buzzing, teeming slope does not know what God might be or encompass.

The branches spike, and their fronds and needles. A low hoo (hoo) wants something of us perhaps. Or perhaps nothing. But we glance that way, pause, and wonder if an owl has read our secret heart.

I, too, Lord, ask who.

For Reflection

- Birds and animals sometimes remind us of what we fear. What in the world of creation do I fear? What in the world of religion might I dread?
- There is serenity in owls. What does their hooting signify to me? Do I consider night life fearsome or friendly?
- How is it that owls have come to symbolize wisdom? What symbolizes wisdom for me?

47.

Works of Wisdom

O Lord, how manifold are your works! In wisdom you have made them all; the earth is full of your creatures. **Ps 104:24**

Psalm 104 is the seagull psalm, the psalm of salt spray, the sky watcher's psalm, the psalm of sun and stars, the psalm of stalkers of prey, the sassafras psalm, the psalm of slithering snakes and winged skates and scattering scree.

Marty Brenner, a seminary professor of biblical studies, calls it a psalm of praise and a masterpiece of world literature. It pronounces blessing upon God and then unfolds why God is great, majestic, and "wrapped in light" (v 2). The psalm proclaims how the waters got into place and how all the world is quenched. It comments on the luminaries above and the alternation of day and night. It tells the fullness with which we are surrounded and how all manner of beings are fed. It moves into a hymn, a highly crafted one. It is deliberate in its effusive catalog of creatures and its cadences of tides and sky, death and life, dawn and dusk. All of creation is God's realm, it says. All of creation, then, must allow God's reign and offer praise.

The psalm ends with its beginning: blessing God. In between, we are invited to amazement at everything. Earth, sea, sky, young water, mountainsides, grassy plains, storks, goats, rabbits, fir trees and cedars appear at God's creative gesture. God shrugs, and a young lion prowls. God yawns, and it retires to its den. God shudders, and the earth quakes; blinks, and smoke fumes from a volcano's mouth.

The psalmist asks only one or two things: that his or her meditations "be pleasing" (v 34) and that "the wicked be no more" (v 35). Evildoing mars the creative order, violates the rhythm and beauty of creation. Willful wrong slurs the word of the Creator Spirit and mars that which God proposes to renew.

Today, God, let me make a list of all things great and small that I notice. Let me see them anew, celebrate life, and spill over to praise.

For Reflection

- J. Baird Callicott has proposed that we need not only a "land ethic" but also a "land aesthetic." How do I opt for beauty? How do I revere the beautiful? When do I meditate upon it?
- The great Pentecost hymn, "Veni, Creator Spiritus"—"Come, Creator Spirit"—has a basis in this psalm's words imploring God to send forth the Spirit to renew the face of the Earth (v 30). What is the state of my faith in the Holy Spirit? Do I relate that faith to budding flowers, peeps in birds' nests, and flowing streams? Why or why not?

48.

Desecrations

Then they attached themselves to the Baal of Peor, and ate sacrifices offered to the dead.
Ps 106:28

Gretel Ehrlich, writing in *Questions of Heaven,* has recounted her disillusioning pilgrimage to Emei Shan, a sacred mountain at what she terms mere "foothills of the Himalayas." She tells us that she found there, on an arduous ascent, tourist traps, cheap imitations of Western taste in filthy hotels, faithless guides, lackluster monks who barely knew how to chant and confessed to taking their vocations as a local job opportunity, a locked and ruined temple, and one ancient lama who rang true. The Maoist Cultural Revolution wrought havoc on the sacred and then had belated regrets. What Ehrlich saw was the government's attempt to acknowledge that loss of spirituality can also mean loss of money, and so it was trying to attract internationals, the intent and the intelligentsia, especially Western Buddhists, to the sites of ancient traditions. The shoddy experience exhausted Ehrlich. What she came to understand is that the climb is at home and within. No hyped-up hike can fulfill spiritual yearning.

It is easy and tempting to bash Communists for atheizing the world, turning the landscape artless, and then trying to recapture a religious market in the way that prostitutes turn tricks. But Americans can hardly deflect blame from themselves for similar desecrations. We've violated Native American burial grounds to build steam plants and shopping malls. We're hell bent on rewriting the laws concerning conservatories and nature preserves if they look promising for oil drilling. We've evaded bids to develop technologies of solar and wind power in order to foster the ever prolonged and enervating courtship with the corporate heads and capital gains associated with fossil fuels. Who cares what bones we trample on? And who measures what growth we stunt?

God-fearing, we like to think ourselves. But our pension plans, I.R.A.s, stock portfolios are built on Baals. We worry over their rises and falls. To what avail? We've long since sacrificed our firstborn and our sacred places to them.

Save me, God, from greed. Give me, source of the sacred and the beautiful, reverence for sacred places and the longings of the human spirit.

For Reflection

- Alternative energies, social principles investments, green planning, and organized resistance of The Way Things Work are often dismissed as lunatic fringe ventures. When have I made a commitment to the less profitable, less popular, more reverent and Earth-friendly in my getting, spending, and investing?
- Is there some place, some way, I can participate in "reconsecrating" some tract of land?

49.

The Wages of Sin?

He turns rivers into a desert, springs of water into thirsty ground, a fruitful land into a salty waste, because of the wickedness of its inhabitants. He turns a desert into pools of water, a parched land into springs of water. Ps 107:33–35

Vice-versa. Hillsides sometimes slide into houses because the houses shouldn't have been built there in the first place. Las Vegas may go dry because deserts are not the most favorable settings for decorative fountains and miles of pipeline. Dams may burst. Rivers may flood and seek their original flood plain, irrespective of our developments and sub-divisions. Wars may lay crops waste. Oil wells may burn. Cancers may grow.

If there is any justice in the turn of events, the perpetrators of waste and weaponry lose. If there is any setting to rights, the poor and the victimized eat and gain.

It isn't always so, though. We hear too often of foodstuffs never getting to famine victims because of a military regime's profiteering and red tape. We know that both sides of conflicts are maimed and die. We see that the poor have the most fragile shelter, the most malnourishing fare, the most meager access to medical care.

Some horrors can be set right only by world courts and war crimes trials. Others can only be rectified by acts of God. Later. À la Lazarus and Dives.

Lord of our ups and downs, our foolishness and rascality and our about-faces toward grace, make sense within us. And grant our just deserts.

For Reflection

- When have I seen the poor surprisingly win and prosper?
- When have I seen sad consequences of short-sightedness and self-gratification?
- What, for me, are the heaviest tolls of war?

50.

Besieged and Bee-Stung

They surrounded me like bees; they blazed like a fire of thorns. **Ps 118:12**

Bees swarm, zoom in aslant, crackle and spit. They can surprise us from a thicket. They can encircle and fluster us from the unwitting overturn of a log.

Bee stings can be deadly. And beekeeping is a dangerous game.

Yet we'll do almost anything for honey.

You are also the God of flowers and clover, queens and drones, hanging hives. Help us to savor the good and sweet and to avoid the madding swarm.

For Reflection

- Bees dipping into the folds of flowers charm us. Bees amassing to mask a human being's face terrify us. What creatures entice and yet also alarm me? Why?
- If I'm allergic, do I, can I, avoid what I'm allergic to? If not, what do I do? How do I sustain a love for God's creatures when I find some capable of deadly harm?

51.

Commands and Limits

I live as an alien in the land; do not hide your commandments from me.
Ps 119:19

Psalm 119 is the longest psalm, offering eight lines for every letter of the Hebrew alphabet and, in each octet, eight synonyms: statutes, precepts, ordinances, word, commandments, judgments, law, decrees. The psalm is a plea for order and sense. It expresses a longing for obedience, the heart and fruit of understanding.

But what does a pine needle know of precept? What does a Connecticut squirrel ken of nature's underlying statutes and decrees? How do the hinges of kelp-strewn mussel and oyster shells give obeisance to God's word?

There are laws of nature, philosophers say, and thus nature does what it will do, in place and on time and in concord with current conditions. There is a natural law, too, written in the heart. It urges us to survive, to propagate, to structure societies, to seek the truth about God. Heeding the promptings of natural law can be possible only if we possess some instinct for the good. It can be practicable only if we have a sense of community and commonality. Such can be had only if we look around and observe what works well and what does harm.

Though we're obviously earthlings, there is something alien and askew about us. We can know that the law of nature requires that we eat, drink, work, excrete, and sleep. Yet we can hold these necessities in abeyance for a time. The law of nature also obliges us to plant, keep, preserve, prepare, stay out of excess cold or heat, take cure when we are ill, and protect our loved ones. These, too, we can omit or ignore. Willy-nilly, we can bend or suspend some of the applications of the law of nature. It isn't surprising, then, that we can also ignore what's prompted by the natural law: that we act reasonably on our own behalf and on behalf of the common good.

The common good, we know, embraces more than our own human selves. We know because an instinct for the good leads us. Following that lead, we find God, and God reminds us that there are commands, ordinances, judgments extrinsic to ourselves, too. These commands simply try to check our perverse inclination to defy the law written in our hearts.

If we insist on acting like aliens, shrinking the world to our small whims and our egocentricities, we get a stern reminder that God's "faithfulness endures to all generations" and that God has "established the Earth and it stands fast" (v 90). Why live harmoniously with and within nature's limits? So that we may utter with some semblance of hope the simple plea: "Let me live..." (v 175), and mean it not only for ourselves.

Do let me live, Lord, thanking, praising, cooperating, sharing. Attentively. Always.

For Reflection

- The natural law tradition is revered in Catholic moral teaching. It guides our principles of social justice and our morality of sexuality and reproduction. What do I know of it?
- If I were setting up some minimal ethical guidelines for living harmoniously with the world of nature, what would they be? Which ones do I most easily follow? What am I more prone to offend?

52.

The Climb

I lift up my eyes to the hills—from where will my help come? **Ps 121:1**

There is something about this psalm. It shows up in the Liturgy of the Hours as the first psalm in Evening Prayer in the Office for the Dead. It also shows up every August 6th, in Evening Prayer for the Feast of the Transfiguration. Grave goes to glory. That would seem to be something of the message of its use.

There is something about hills and mountains, too. They beckon us to climb. They symbolize the desires we hope to attain yet know that a grueling task, with ropes and cleated shoes and spikes, may be before us. They're the figure for spiritual journeys, East and West, and the sites for visions of God. Nebo, Sinai, Tabor. And so many of the psalms are prefixed "A Song of Ascents."

What about the climb? What about its God-ward quality? The peak may be snow-capped or wreathed in clouds. We're promised that our feet won't slip, that there will be shade, that the light won't be blinding. Not, at least, on the spiritual journey.

The first secret of the climb, then, is trust. The second secret is that wherever the climb leads—to ecstasy, to transfiguration, or to death—it is accomplished step by step, with a straining and a yearning ever up.

Be my staff and guy-line, God, when and where I climb.

For Reflection

- St. Bonaventure's *The Ascent of the Mind to God*, St. John of the Cross's *Ascent of Mount Carmel*, Thomas Merton's *The Seven Storey Mountain*, Hannah Hunnard's *Hinds Feet on High Places*, and the Zen sayings of Santoka Taneda collected as *Mountain Tasting*: these are just a few mountainous spiritual works. How is my own spiritual journey like climbing a mountain? Where am I now?

- What physical mountains have I ascended (by foot, by lift, by incline, by car, by bus)? Did the journey seem perilous at any point? What beauty did it reveal?

53.

Duckwatch

We have escaped like a bird from the snare of the fowlers; the snare is broken, and we have escaped. **Ps 124:7**

Sometimes we just want one last peek at the ducks. We're told not to feed them, because staying too well fed distracts them from migration. But it's a temptation—to establish a relationship, to feel that welcome flurry, if we but proffer some bread crumbs.

Sometimes we just want one last soak of late afternoon sun. In a chilly time, a walk where shafts of warmth from the west can strike us feels healthful, energizing, cozy as a hint of home fire yet freely outside.

So we stroll the marina. We squawk in whispers to the ducks. We sidle a hand into a small bag. We pop a few crumbs into the water. They scurry, dip, nod their mallard beaks in gratitude. The sun is still up, though the air is cool.

And they're still here.

One or two others besides ourselves might be feeding them. We've escaped detection and censure, so far.

Will our ducks, though, escape winter?

I don't imagine, God, that anyone has ever confessed to feeding ducks where it is prohibited. But help me remember that my incautious action, my entertainment, my small selfishness, can break their patterns and stifle their inner compasses. Give me the virtue of letting your waterfowl go their way.

For Reflection

- Cartoon mice, ducks, coyotes, rabbits, moose, squirrels, dogs, pigs, and cats have entertained us as children. What do we still have to learn about the real things? Have the artifices of child's play and cartoons robbed us of realism about the world of birds, fish, rodents, and mammals? Are we sinning against them by regarding them as cute and ours?

54.

Into the Everlasting

Your children will be like olive shoots around your table. **Ps 128:3**

"If there is life after the earth-life, will you come with me?" That is the opening question in the title prose-poem of Mary Oliver's *West Wind* collection. What comes after? To whom or what do we go? Are there companions for our journey? The questions are universal and ageless.

We wonder, too, what remains. Who is left? What have we handed on and to whom? We wish not only to live on in eternity but also to live on here on Earth. We touch someone in a caring ministry, perhaps. We teach someone a timeless truth, a vital life lesson. We decorate some corner with our art or inscribe a love in poetry. We have children, and they have children, and they have children, and something of us goes on. We build something, start something, change something, and it matters. Someone, we hope, remembers our name for one paltry good deed.

What comes next, here or there? We tend to think in more populous terms, in categories of human and divine relations. But Oliver, ever the lover of nature, would count the olive shoots, too, along with the children. If they did not matter, no one would have planted them. So, she talks to a nameless someone in "West Wind," to a young person. But she also, throughout her poetry, speaks to and about butterflies, oaks, hawks, snakes shedding their skins, corn stalks, wild turkeys, beech trees, the household dogs, snowflakes, and beach plums. Christianity is cocksure we don't take them with us. They don't have immortal souls, the tradition says. But....

But they are imprinted in human memory. Landscape, the living creatures, and the weathers of our bioregions are formative of who we are. When I meet God face to face it will be as an "I" shaped by the New York City skyline, a New Jersey barrier island, central Pennsylvania's farms and coal fields and mountains, and Michigan's lakes. I take with me memories of house sparrows, gulls and terns, ring-necked pheasants, and great blue herons. They become at least a part of who I am. I also bear, I dare say, imprints of a grape arbor, dune grass, crabapple trees, and purple loosestrife on my being, just as truly as I carry the lesions of human hurts and the heartwarmth of human friendship and love wherever I go.

"Will you come with me?" the poet asks. In one way or another, surely. No matter who the "you" of the poem are.

God of wherever I am, bless abundantly wherever I've been. Bless, too, where I shall be with you, and with all who have formed and mattered in me.

For Reflection

- Winifred Gallagher and Robert Hamma have developed theories of how we are shaped, how our personalities are formed and transformed, by landscape. Does a "big sky" person really differ vastly from someone born and bred by a seaside? Does desert shape a consciousness different from one developed in the Appalachians? Does Vermont affect its citizens differently from the way Missouri does? Give illustrations.

- What selves, human and nonhuman, have molded your personality? Your faith?

55.

Offering Creation

How very good and pleasant it is when kindred live together in unity! It is like the precious oil on the head running down upon the beard, on the beard of Aaron. **Ps 133:2**

The Orthodox view of humanity's relation to the created world is a priestly one. The human being receives created goods as gifts from God. Having received gifts, the human person offers them back, pledging to use them for well-being, for universal charity. Created goods are anointed and blessed, then they are given out for nourishing, strengthening, healing. Creatures, in this way, are regarded as sacramental. They are occasions of encounter with God. They effect a positive change in the recipient, the beholder. They are a sign of unity, a sign of blessing, sign of God's abundance, but, as sacrament, they also make unity, blessing, and abundance happen.

Thus, anything in creation can be regarded as an icon, not one that we've written, but one crafted by angelic powers. The icon is beautiful and artful in itself, but it also opens a window unto God. The brightness of the icon draws us to Light.

Anything in creation can be regarded as holy. We can swing incense to it, around it, circling it, and lifting it up. Anything made by God can be seen as wine, cubes of bread, water of blessing, holy oil. Whatever holds sacramental elements must be a precious vessel, an elegant flask, a jeweled chalice, a glistening plate. We humans are, then, both priest and precious vessel.

It is no surprise, then, that the Orthodox understand it not only as a moral act but also as an act of adoration to protect the fields and forests of Cyprus, to assure that its waters flow fresh and pure.

Creator God, I praise and honor you in the way I receive your gifts. I offer them to you, bless them, hold them precious, and ask that I always use them as blessing and benefit.

For Reflection

- If we were to treat our yards, gardens, vacant lots, woodlands, beaches as holy places, as sanctuaries, what would we be doing differently?

56.

≈·⊃·≈

Acts of Love

O give thanks to the Lord...who alone does great wonders, for his steadfast love endures forever; who by understanding made the heavens, for his steadfast love endures forever; who spread out the earth on the waters, for his steadfast love endures forever. Ps 136:3–6

God makes love to us in the lap of water and the lay of the land. There are moments, however, when we're too harried to notice beauty, too urgent and rushed to be grateful. There is something about our lives—the pressures of work, the demands of our belongings, the needs (real or imagined) of families and friends, the stress of our ambitions, the uncertainties of health, weather, the economy, and the future—something that unbalances us. Something, anything, everything sends us careening through our lives. God, meanwhile, waits for us to slow down, catch our breath, notice something, and speak a small word of thanks.

God wants to be the wind, stirring the curtains at a frost-crackled window open a mere half inch. God wants to signal us to watch the lift of yellow leaves, a rakeful at a time, to form a mulch pile, then downturn into soil.

God wants to be the sun, casting shine relentlessly, melting frost from morning's shrubs and softening stiffened limbs. God wants to warm each sunrise with spectacle and sheen and turn each sunset into fireworks that leave us gasping, gasping with delight.

God wants to stun us with a touch of creek flowing on our toes, a raindrop that goes splat on the back of our hands, a spin of flower petals and leaves hustled and then dropped in a wind rush.

God wants us sometimes to stop, to consider the lilies of the field and the birds of the air, to remember steadfast love.

O God of loveliness, let me heed the signs that tell me to yield. Give me eyes to see with, ears to hear with, a heart to thank with. And continue to love me, please.

For Reflection

- Judy Cannato, writing in *Quantum Grace*, speaks of how we can be "owned by our weariness." We're so exhausted and strained by sleep deprivation and the daily round that we forget to be grateful. We miss the small miracles of life and day. What specific steps must I take to become more attentive and less weary? When do I plan to start—to take the first step?

57.

Birthright

For it was you who formed my inward parts; you knit me together in my mother's womb.
Ps 139:13

The late Carl Sagan delighted in reminding us that we are all made of "starstuff." The molecules that form blood, bone, and brain arose in cosmic explosions. The elemental genetic material at our beginning is held in common with all manner of creatures. Ninety-nine percent of our genetic makeup is also found in chimpanzees. Some people believe our menstrual periods keep pace with the phases of the moon and the tides. While humans can procreate without being "in heat" or having seasons for "rutting," people often need mild temperatures, low light, tasty but not over-abundant food, and sips of fine wine to get them going. Our birth, our growth, our health, our talents, our tendencies, our longevity are born in an intricate mix of nature and nurture. No matter how old we are, we are in many ways ancient. Some of our iron, some of our zinc, some of our phosphorus, some of our potassium goes back not only centuries but millennia. We're water and mulch, and we sprinkle salt when we sweat or cry.

The discoveries of the double helix of DNA and of the human genome project haven't, though, really cracked our code. Nor has the talk of the possibility of cloning us. Psychoanalysis and sociological profiles have not yet explained why some persons build rockets and some sail in lit boats along shores at night, why some fashion pottery with damp, clayed hands and others spank, why some sing and others smoke, why this one falls in love with that one and another alienates a whole world.

In a universe billions of years old bearing billions of galaxies, we can feel dwarfed, inconsequential, swallowed up in mysteries that really don't matter. Faith, though, speaks of a cosmic One who knows us, individually and personally, despite our multiplicity and diversity, through eons of time.

Against all odds, Moses, David, the prophets, Elizabeth, Mary, Jesus, all the great saints and mystics, urge that we are known and wonderful, knowingly begotten rather than randomly produced, fascinatingly free yet also destined. There's nowhere to go that the Creator isn't. Amid infinite mystery, we find that there is nowhere in which we can be unknown.

Hear me, God, when I too can pray that I am "fearfully and wonderfully made." Let me pray it with trust and surrender.

For Reflection

- Omniscience can be a frightening concept. What fears do I have about being known—by God or by anyone?
- What don't I understand about myself and wish I did?
- When can I praise God genuinely, acknowledging that "I am fearfully and wonderfully made" (v 14)?

58.

❧❧❧

Traps, Nets, and Snares

The arrogant have hidden a trap for me, and with cords they have spread a net, along the road they have set snares for me. **Ps 140:5**

The *Catechism of the Catholic Church* condemns the abuse and mistreatment of animals. It denounces cruelty to them under the seventh commandment, which suggests that not everything is ours simply because we have power over it. Possession (of a pet, of zoo animals, of something raised in a laboratory) is not license to mutilate or inflict pain. The condemnation is there for a reason, of course. The church would not have to denounce cruelty to animals if there were not so much of it around. Cock or dog-fighting, fox hunts, pigeon shoots, cosmetic testing, and the harvesting of musk for human scents can be bloody and disabling. Raising veal for the tender palate requires the confinement of calves in narrow stalls (to thwart muscle development) and diets planned with anemia in mind. The market for ivory, we're told, has resulted in shoot-to-kill legislation against poachers. The poacher, a person, can be killed for what he or she does to elephants.

One of the reasons the church has long condemned cruelty to animals (back to the time of Thomas Aquinas, at least) is its sense that violence against one species easily opens the way to violence against others.

Inflicting needless pain on a pet or otherwise "owned" animal—or one in the wild—is sadistic and, thus, a prediction of more sadism to come.

Those of us who have lived in rural areas or large houses know, however, that mice like peanut butter as much as cheese, that bats cannot always be induced to follow air currents out open windows, and that groundhogs and moles can overrun and undermine our yards. Traps, nets, poisons, and gunshots are often what we resort to. They're efficient and solve our animal problems.

Dealing with "varmints" and "pests" puts us in an area of moral ambiguity, it seems, even those of us who love our household Bichons, canaries, and cottontail rabbits. The question for us is when and how we apply standards requiring us to minimize pain and to renounce anything that smacks of cruelty, taunting, crazing animals.

We're invited to think again about how casual attitudes toward the pain of animals, about how our haste to dispatch them, can predispose us to casual attitudes toward fighting, toward crime. We may find ourselves sliding easily from the shrug over the for-profit gamelands that offer up trophy boars, zebras, and ibis to shrugs over acts of war.

We may find ourselves caught in traps, nets, and snares of our own senselessness.

God of mercy, stay my hand from cruelty. Let me refrain from anything that causes pain and pathos that is not curative. Give me the tenderness to know when I'm called to intervene, heal, challenge any kind of violence.

For Reflection

- Pax Christi U.S.A. has promoted a vow of nonviolence. Its focus, of course, is on renouncing all human-to-human violence. Could I make such a vow? Why or why not?
- What violence or cruelty do I accept as necessary?
- In what traps, nets, or snares do I see the American public caught? To what extent am I a participant?

59.

Pure Desires

The eyes of all look to you, and you give them their food in due season. You open your hand, satisfying the desire of every living thing. **Ps 145:15–16**

Single-mindedness, presence to things present, a passion for the transcendent, and a heart for the world are all qualities possessed by the men and women profiled in Winifred Gallagher's *Spiritual Genius*. They're all stellar figures: a brother laboring among India's "unreached" to help them develop self-sufficiency; a rabbi who pores over the texts of the Kabbalah and unlocks its mysticism for sophisticated New Yorkers and Bostonians; a Buddhist nun whose secluded and ceremonial life in Tibet radiates to the West; a nurse who, after long service in Bangladesh, finds a home among the Carmelites. Each of these—like any prophet, saint, or great reformer—is remarkable for his or her focus. Remarkable, too, is the zeal and the ability to suspend attention to personal pain which characterizes each of them. Life is journey, inward or outward, and mission, and that is what drives each one.

None of us who lead have the gifts to measure our personal worth by the amount of our properties, or the growth of our investments. None worries unduly about pensions or retirement funds. Each one is marked by our ability to attend to the day's gifts and to approach human need with open hands and humility. An irrevocable view of life as a gift and spiritual realism would seem to be the sum of the attitudes and activities of those Gallagher calls "geniuses" of the spiritual realm. Each of her heroes treats life as gratuitous, as a mystery to be explored, a journey to be traveled, a treasure to be held as sacred. Each knows that his or her life is immersed in the holy, however unnamable that may be. Each one also knows that his or her life is set at the service of humanity, in whatever circle of influence humanity may appear. Each, too, lives lightly on the land.

Psalm 145 celebrates the majesty, awesomeness, glory of the Holy. It exults in life and asks nothing but the capacity to keep on giving thanks. The psalm celebrates purity of desire, purity of heart, and unshakable confidence. It suggests that all of us can sing if we allow ourselves to see with the eyes of the ordinary mystic, the everyday saint.

A panorama unfolds before every human life. It is ours simply to see and embrace.

God, enlarge my heart and focus my vision so that I may see goodness and glory. Always. And with thanks.

For Reflection

- History is marked and changed by the lives of saints and martyrs. Who are some of the saints and martyrs who have affected the world during my lifetime? What passions drove them? What passions drive me?
- Chico Mendes is perhaps the first of the world's known eco-martyrs. What can I learn from this Brazilian?
- So I'm not a "spiritual genius." What homeground good can I do in a bigger way than I am doing now? What adjustments to my typical seeing, thinking, and doing would free me for greater love and gratitude?

60.

❧

Caritas for All Creation

He heals the brokenhearted, and binds up their wounds. He determines the number of the stars; he gives to all of them their names...He gives to the animals their food, and to the young ravens when they cry. **Ps 147:3–4,9**

Hammonasset State Park in Connecticut is still worn by winter in early April. The pine and scrub evergreen have all been beaten eastward. The thickets of berry bush and bramble are a stubby, prickly, dark brown. The sea grass, some of it cracked in half, is a washed-out yellow, almost the color of sand. And the sand has drifted over boardwalk, pathway, pavilion steps. The West Beach, though, is busy, as long as there is sun. Even if it's still a winter coat weekend, elderly couples, adamant middle-aged power walkers, parents with young children all come. A lacrosse team whacks its way only yards from the beach. Park entry is still free, and will be for weeks.

Tufts of white feathers are sprinkled across one lot, where some scramble between species must have taken place. The occasional crow waddles out from a bush and doesn't flutter a wing at the sight of a human. There are pickings here. Human trash from a chill picnic; snack leavings from an SUV's litter bag. Dogs bark merrily on long leashes. And in the barely occupied parking lots, the gulls swoop and cartwheel in pre-summer glee.

The quiescent world is outing. Cold days are numbered. Summer people may molest some habitats, but they bring all the square meals a gull can peck. If fish are scant or slim, trail mix, potato chips, and Chex are fillers.

A mom, a dad, a young girl, all in hiking shoes, enter the park and walk toward the windy beach at high tide. They're carrying a kite. It's shaped like a shark.

And the play goes on.

It is Sunday.

Sabbath God, thank you for days of revels. Thank you for days when the promise of spring draws me to long shores, to bird play, to wind and sunny sea. Help me remember your rhythms, the upstarts and rests.

For Reflection

- Where have I seen nature in a feeding frenzy? Where have I seen people most at ease?
- If I were to write a love psalm, celebrating creatures together on a day of play, how would it go?

61.

Unbounded Praise

Praise the Lord from the earth, you sea monsters and all deeps, fire and hail, snow and frost, stormy wind fulfilling his command! Ps 148:7–8

The highest form of prayer, we're told, is praise. It's what angelic choirs do. It's what great saints do. All is Alleluia, O Happy Day, Wonderful and Great, Hip Hip Hooray! Praise celebrates what is. Praise revels and enjoys. Praise flaps its wings like loons exulting in a smooth high tide. Praise waves palm branches to welcome what is and what's next. Praise holds its breath, then goes "Aah" at a shower of shooting stars.

Curiously enough, the psalmist claims that it is not only those gifted with language and intellect who praise. Living, breathing things do. The elements do. The idea seems to be that a creature's simply being what it is and fulfilling what it is meant to be is in itself an act of praise.

We can think of praise simply as the pure expression of *raison d'être*: reason for being. It arises from an inherent sense of direction, some intrinsic way of interacting, responding, adapting, regrouping, affecting, offering up whatever one is.

The psalmist sees the web of life as a chorus of praise. Kings and young women, fruit trees and cattle, rainwater and wind, the moon and spinning invisible things are all summoned to sing. Their song is their very being. Carrying out their genetic code, acting on opportunities, pursuing God-given drives, being uniquely for and being uniquely with are their refrains.

What glory does God get from all this? The glory of conducting unseen and producing what the medievals called the harmony of the spheres.

Raise my one small voice, God, and let it, too, harmonize.

For Reflection

- Do we find it strange to think of nonhuman creatures offering praise, having a form of prayer? What difference would it make—to us and in us—if we saw them that way?
- If we repeat the "Canticle of the Sun" by St. Francis of Assisi side by side with this psalm, what similarities do we find? What differences?
- Some contemporary meditative recordings and Paul Winter's *Missa Gaia* include loon cries, wolf howls, the beat of whales, the rattle of rainsticks, the sounds of water lapping in their musical scores. How am I affected by such sound effects introduced into musical compositions?

62.

❧❧❧

And in the End, Praise

Let everything that breathes praise the Lord! **Ps 150:6**

Praise of the creator, exultation in the artisan of the universe, can and ought to, says the psalmist, happen everywhere: in religious places (the "sanctuary"), under the skies (the "firmament"). Music, rousing and boisterous, vital and vigorous, is a response to the goodness of life itself, an appropriate expression of Earth-energy.

The very fact that we breathe is also music and praise. It is no mistake that the same Hebrew word, *ru'ah*, can mean breath, wind, or Spirit. It is no mistake that the Greek word *pneuma* can mean air, breath, or the spiritual. Wind wakes the waters at creation (Gen 1;2). And the Spirit, like a battering wind, shakes the house of prayer at Pentecost and gives the stunned and silent their voices (Acts 2).

John Calvin, in his *Institutes of the Christian Religion*, has remarked that every creature bears the "unmistakable marks" and the "sparks" of God's glory (I v 1). All creatures, Calvin says, exhibit something of God's wisdom, justice, goodness, and power (I xiv 21).

Thomas Aquinas, as noted earlier in this collection, has similarly declared, in the *Summa Theologica*, that "in all creatures there is found the trace of the Trinity" (I 45 7). He has also asserted that creaturely

139

diversity is crucial to the fuller revelation of "the divine goodness" (I 47 1). Each creature has, says Thomas, its own "proper act and perfection," its own reason for being, and all together contribute to "the perfection of the entire universe" (I 65 2).

Both Aquinas and Calvin perceive all creatures as, in their own unique ways, revealing something of God's splendor. But both stop short of describing creatures as somehow themselves offering prayer or praise.

The psalmist, as we have already seen, goes farther. As the ancient celebrant of God stared into the night sky, he saw that the very act of breathing in harmony with God's creative word was itself praise. The beat of life sings both of God and to God simultaneously.

For us, this may mean that the Christian dictum to "pray always" can be realized so very, very easily.

To breathe as long as there is breath can be an offer of adoration. Merely to be—and to be attuned to the Spirit that awakens winds and waters and all the multitude of beings—can be our speaking of and to the God who is pure Being. We may form words, craft poems, shape hymnic tones, add mysteries to the rosary, plan elaborate novenas, or test new liturgical prayers, but, in the end, God wants only the air that we are, in and out, the air that makes our blood dance.

Creator God, take every breath of mine, every inhalation and exhalation of everything that lives, every sound and sigh of the universe as a hymn of praise. Take our being into yours with every amen, every alleluia. Selah.

For Reflection

- In his great *Hymn of the Universe*, Teilhard de Chardin offers "The Mass on the World." In the midst of its prayer of offering, he asserts: "In the beginning there were not coldness and darkness. There was the Fire." For Teilhard, that Fire is what blazes in the very "heart of the world." What cosmic fire blazes in me? What gives that fire the air it needs? When have I been on fire, and for what? How might my prayer, my very life, aerate? How might I become fire?

For Further Reading

On ecology, landscape, eco-ethics, ecotheology and ecospirituality

Berry, Thomas, C.P., with Thomas Clarke, S. J. *Befriending the Earth: A Theology Of Reconciliation Between Humans and the Earth.* Ed. Stephen Dunn, C. P. and Anne Lonergan. Mystic: Twenty-Third Publications, 1991.

Camara, Dom Helder. *Sister Earth: Creation, Ecology, and the Spirit.* Hyde Park: New City Press, 1995.

Barad, Judith. *Aquinas on the Nature and Treatment of Animals.* San Francisco: International Scholars Publications, 1995.

Callicott, J. Baird. *In Defense of the Land Ethic: Essays in Environmental Philosophy.* Albany: State University of New York Press, 1989.

Carson, Rachel. *Silent Spring.* New York: Houghton Mifflin, 1962.

Christiansen, Drew, S.J., and Walter Grazer. *"And God Saw That It Was Good": Catholic Theology and the Environment.* Washington: United States Catholic Conference, 1996.

Devall, Bill and George Sessions. *Deep Ecology: Living as if Nature Mattered.* Salt Lake City: Gibbs M. Smith, 1985.

Dempsey, Carol J. and Russell A. Butkus, eds. *All Creation Is Groaning: An Interdisciplinary Vision for Life in a Sacred Universe*. Collegeville: Liturgical Press, 1999.

Dillard, Annie. *Pilgrim at Tinker Creek*. In *Three by Annie Dillard*. New York: Harper Collins, 1990.

———. *Holy the Firm*. New York: Harper and Row, 1977.

Dowd, Michael. *Earthspirit: A Handbook for Nurturing an Ecological Christianity*, Mystic: Twenty-Third Publications, 1991.

Ehrlich, Gretel. *A Match to the Heart*. New York: Penguin Books, 1994.

———. *Questions of Heaven: The Chinese Journeys of an American Buddhist*. Boston: Beacon Press, 1997.

Flader, Susan L. *Thinking Like a Mountain: Aldo Leopold and the Evolution of an Ecological Attitude toward Deer, Wolves, and Forests*. Columbia: University of Missouri Press, 1974.

Hamma, Robert M. *Landscapes of the Soul: A Spirituality of Place*. Notre Dame: Ave, Maria Press, 1999.

Jensen, Derrick. *Listening to the Land: Conversations about Nature, Culture, and Eros*. San Francisco: Sierra Club Books, 1995.

Johnson, Elizabeth A. *Women, Earth, and Creator Spirit*. New York: Paulist Press, 1993.

La Chance, Albert J. and John E. Carroll, eds. *Embracing Earth: Catholic Approaches to Ecology*. Maryknoll: Orbis Press, 1994.

Leopold, Aldo. *A Sand County Almanac and Sketches Here and There*. New York, Oxford University Press, 1949; reprint, 1989.

Linzey, Andrew. *Animal Theology*. Chicago: University of Illinois Press, 1994.

———. *Animal Gospel*. Louisville: Westminster John Knox Press, 1998.

Lopez, Barry. *Of Wolves and Men*. New York: Simon and Schuster, 1978.

Lovelock, James. *Gaia: A New Look at Life on Earth*. New York: Oxford University Press, 1979; reprint, 1987.

Masson, Jeffrey Moussaieff and Susan McCarthy. *When Elephants Weep: The Emotional Lives of Animals*. New York: Dell Publishing, 1995.

Matthews, Anne. *Wild Nights: Nature Returns to the City*. New York: North Point Press, 2001.

May, Roy. *Ética y Medio Ambiente: Hacia Una Vida Sostenible*. San Jose: Editorial Departamento Ecumenico de Investigaciones, 2002.

Merton, Thomas. *When the Trees Say Nothing*, ed. Kathleen Deignan. Notre Dame: Sorin Books, 2003.

Nothwehr, Dawn M., O.S.F. *Theology of the Environment: An Introductory Reader*. Quincy: Franciscan Press, 2002.

Presbyterian Eco-Justice Task Force. *Keeping and Healing the Creation*. Louisville: Presbyterian Church (U.S.A.), 1989.

Singer, Peter, ed. *Ethics*. New York: Oxford University Press, 1994.

Smith, Pamela. *What Are They Saying About Environmental Ethics?* New York: Paulist Press, 1997.

So That All God's Creation Might Live: The Orthodox Church Responds to the Ecological Crisis. Constantinople: Ecumenical Patriarchate, 1992.

Starke, Linda, ed. *State of the World 2003*. New York: W. W. Norton (Worldwatch), 2003

Van Wensveen, Louke. *Dirty Virtues: The Emergence of Ecological Virtue Ethics*. Amherst: Humanity Books, 2000.

White, Lynn, Jr. "The Historical Roots of Our Ecologic Crisis." In *Western Man and Environmental Ethics*, ed. Ian G. Barbour. Reading: Addison-Wesley Publishing Company, 1973.

On the psalms, prayer, poetry, and God-thoughts

Cannato, Judy. *Quantum Grace: Lenten Reflections on Creation and Connectedness.*, Notre Dame: Ave Maria Press, 2003.

Cleary, William. *How the Wild Things Pray*. Leavenworth: Forest of Peace, 1999.

Craghan, John F. *Psalms for All Seasons*. Collegeville: Liturgical Press, 1993.

Gallagher, Winifred. *Spiritual Genius: The Mastery of Life's Meaning*. New York: Random House, 2001.

Gutierrez, Gustavo. *The God of Life*. Trans. Matthew J. O'Connell. Maryknoll: Orbis Books, 1991.

Kraus, Hans-Joachim. *Theology of the Psalms*. Trans. Keith Crim. Minneapolis: Fortress Press, 1992.

Kushner, Harold S. *When Bad Things Happen to Good People*. New York: Avon Books, 1981.

LaCugna, Catherine Mowry. *God for Us: The Trinity and Christian Life*. San Francisco: Harper San Francisco, 1991.

Oliver, Mary. *West Wind*. New York: Houghton Mifflin Company, 1997.

Quesson, Noel. *The Spirit of the Psalms*. Trans., ed. Marie-France Curtin. New York: Paulist Press, 1990.

Reid, Stephen Breck. *Listening In: A Multicultural Reading of the Psalms*. Nashville: Abingdon Press, 1997.

Schaper, Donna. *Sabbath Sense: A Spiritual Antidote for the Overworked*. Philadelphia: Innisfree Press, 1997.

Simsic, Wayne. *Natural Prayer: Encountering God in Nature*. Mystic: Twenty-Third Publications, 1991.

Stevens, John, trans. and ed. *Mountain Tasting: Zen Haiku* by Santoka Taneda. New York: Weatherhill, 1982.

Valles, Carlos G., S.J. *Psalms for Contemplation*. Chicago: Loyola University Press, 1990.

Van Doren, Mark and Maurice Samuel. *The Book of Praise: Dialogues on the Psalms*. Ed. Edith Samuel. New York: John Day Company, 1975.